BACK ROADS AND
COUNTRY COOKING

BACK ROADS
AND
COUNTRY
COOKING

Sara Waxman

McClelland and Stewart

The Canadian Publishers
McClelland and Stewart Limited
25 Hollinger Road, Toronto M4B 3G2

Canadian Cataloguing in Publication Data

Waxman, Sara
  Back roads and country cooking

Includes index.
ISBN 0-7710-8864-7

1. Cookery, Canadian. 2. Cookery — Ontario.
I. Title.

TX715.W39 1985   641.59713   C85-099685-6

Printed and bound in Canada by Gagné Ltd.

To my family,
Al, Tobaron, and Adam,
and to epicures
everywhere who shared
their recipes with me

Acknowledgements

I am grateful to all those who helped with the preparation of this book and for their generous consideration.

With first-class courtesy, Nordair carried me cheerfully, safely, and promptly to Thunder Bay, Sault Ste. Marie, Ottawa, and Dryden. We were on the same wave length. As I scoured the land for our best foods, Nordair was serving them in the air: Ontario's wines, dewy fresh produce, and delicious local meats and poultry.

The patient kitchen and dining-room staff of the Delta Chelsea Inn in Toronto helped me test, adapt, and taste my recipes.

The Ministry of Tourism and Recreation gave advice and encouragement, and corroborated my belief that there is wonderful adventure past the city limits.

The Ontario Motor League provided accurate maps and travel routes to the highways and byways – and not once did I get lost.

The Bicentennial Commission provided the initial inspiration for the book.

At the end of the road, carved out of the wilderness, was Minaki Lodge, a luxurious northern hideaway and a fitting end to an unforgettable journey. There, cocktails are served on a tiny, unspoiled out-island, and a piper in full highland regalia announces dinner, as he glides by in an Indian canoe. Modern man's pursuit of comfort and luxury is juxtaposed against the incredible beauty of the north.

Cover:

Polo/Ralph Lauren at Hazelton Lanes, Toronto, supplied separates for my elegant country look from their Chintz Collection, and European Jewellery, Toronto, provided the pearls that "go with everything." Skip Dean took the picture.

Illustrations:

The charming illustrations that introduce each chapter were rendered by Louisa Varalta.

Contents

Introduction

The charm of rural life is wasted on me. I was brought up on a farm, on the flat Manitoba prairie, and I figure I've seen enough grass, trees, and waving wheatfields, thank you. Empty spaces make me nervous. To feel secure I need to be surrounded by glass-and-steel skyscrapers, to have the concrete beneath my feet, and to know that there's an all-night drugstore on the corner.

But as the first trilliums push through the sun-warmed soil, everyone I know starts talking about "the country," about opening the cottage, about spending a weekend at a remote village inn, or about going on a picnic. They speak poetically about the sunrise, the smell of clover in the air, the relaxing pace, and, of course, that fine country cooking.

Enthusiasm is contagious. So I decided to make my own voyage of discovery: I embarked on a twenty-thousand-mile culinary odyssey that took me to the far corners of the vast province of Ontario. I'd already seen most of the main events, like Niagara Falls, the Stratford and Shaw drama festivals, Oktoberfest in Kitchener-Waterloo, and the wineries of Niagara-on-the-Lake. I planned an epicurean tour through the province, region by region.

I tasted country cooking in restaurants converted from grist mills, flour mills, prohibition-era bootleggers' headquarters, octagonal barns (so the devil can't corner you), tailor shops, stables, stone castles, dance halls, rooming houses, and millionaires' mansions. I was caught in rainstorms in Cobourg, Thessalon, Picton, and Thunder Bay; in a convertible, I got a glorious suntan on the picturesque back roads of Bath, Trout Creek, Nolalu, and Whitefish Falls. I saw the awesome, rugged beauty of the Great Lakes and the far north through the windows of a Nordair jet. I discovered pheasant in Point Pelee, perch in Port Dover, Canada goose and wild duck on Manitoulin Island, caviar in Sturgeon Falls, pickerel in Kenora, apples, peaches, and pears in the fruit belt, red-skinned peanuts in Ayre, chèvre (goat cheese) in Elmira and the Cheddars at Eldorado, Balderson, and Ingersoll; I picked wild blueberries, Saskatoon berries, and raspberries in North Bay; I inhaled the aroma of chocolate from the Hershey plant in Smiths Falls; I visited luxurious fishing camps in Dryden, with dining rooms that would make city gourmet cafés hang their heads in shame. I sampled reindeer steak, brisket of beaver, bear chops, and grouse *en cocotte*, and was overwhelmed by the grandeur of Minaki Lodge, set like a jewel in a wilderness of evergreens and crystal lakes.

More than a thousand recipes were sent to me from every corner of Ontario, and I received some from as far away as British Columbia and Nova Scotia. Men and women were proud to share their families' favourite foods with others, foods they'd tasted since childhood, foods that had been brought, by their parents or grandparents, to this country. It was a delicious road I followed, to choose those dishes included in this book. Each recipe was given careful consideration, and those that were chosen were tested and adapted to suit today's modern kitchens. They make use of the bountiful produce of the province – the fruits and vegetables, the meats, fish, and game. Others represent foods served in the many restaurants of the province.

Toronto's Delta Chelsea Inn offered me the assistance of their chefs Dominic Zoffranieri and Brian Philips. Their professional equipment is a far cry from my little kitchen. The grills, deep-fryer, and salamander broiler were hot enough to frizzle my eyelashes; the countertop stove so high I had to stand on a box; the commercial skillets so heavy I could barely lift them with both hands; but the staff co-operated – rescuing me from what could have been situation comedy. Their kitchen is every cook's "dream come true" – every ingredient, every spice, and every utensil available at my fingertips. I could hardly wait until it was time for me to start "work" each day. And the Chelsea's executive chef, Dominic Zoffranieri, has ESP with food. He can look at a pie and say, "Too much cream, not enough egg," or taste a sauce and know instinctively which component is off-balance. With his advice I modified and adapted each recipe.

Now we can all share these delicious and hearty foods. They prove that Ontario is not only "a place to stand and a place to grow" – it's also a place to eat! A paradise for food-lovers. An extraordinary open-air supermarket of the finest edibles nature has to offer – that's Ontario.

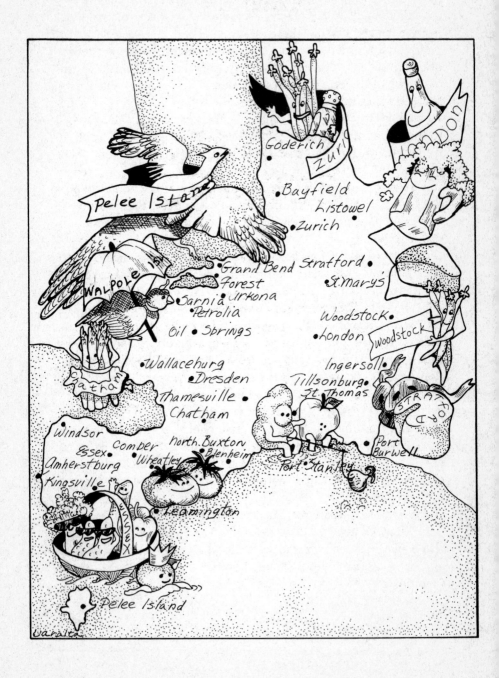

10

CHAPTER 1

SOUTHERN EXPOSURE

*This pastoral landscape, dotted by
historical towns and villages, sits like a
giant vegetable garden bordered by sparkling
lakes: Huron, St. Clair, and Erie. The rolling farmland
is home to herds of dairy and beef cattle – the basis of a
cheese industry that has thrived here since
the nineteenth century.*

Recipes

Restaurants of the Region

AMHERSTBURG

Ducks on the Roof • An old hunting lodge with a homey atmosphere, specializing in game, duckling, rabbit, and pheasant

BAYFIELD

Little Inn • Fresh fish and roast beef

The Red Pump • Elegant country pine

LONDON

Auberge de Petit Prince • Formal, splendid menu

Friars • An exciting salad bar, steaks, and chicken

Gabriele's • Sophisticated "nouvelle" menu and large wine list

Tartan Snack Bar • Hot dogs, hamburgers, and sandwiches with amazing pickles and relishes

MORRISTON

Envers • A pretty stone cottage with a profusion of flowers and a delightful menu

NEW DUNDEE

The Emporium • Scottish-style afternoon tea

PORT STANLEY

Kettle Creek Inn • Meat and fish menu

SHREWSBURY

Whites Motel • Southern fried chicken and biscuits

STRATFORD

The Church • Extravagant, formal "nouvelle" dining

The Old Prune • Stylishly pretty; light meals

Rundles • Inventive, chic, and lovely

The Sun Room • A sunny bistro menu

WINDSOR

Auberge de la Bastile • Dignified fine dining

Chez Vin • A wine bar with food

Cooks Shop • Neapolitan cooking. Choose your own fish for grilling. Excellent fresh pasta

La Cuisine • Charming open kitchen. Informal French cuisine

The Corner Lunch Bar • Cabbage rolls, perogis, good Polish cooking

The Himalaya • Indian meals in an exotic setting

The Hi-Way • Big helpings, family style

The Orient Express • Eclectic oriental dining, Japanese and Chinese

Wong's • Excellent Chinese cooking

Filleted Trout with Almonds

"It's cold up in Canada. Where's your south?" a Hollywood actress asked me.

I answered that Canada spread in only three directions: mostly north, then fairly equally east and west.

Today, I would answer that we do have a south. Pelee Island, a short ferry ride from Point Pelee, is a veritable Garden of Eden, with grape-vines, berry bushes, and thousands of pheasants. Surrounded by the waters of Lake Erie, which teem with fish, it's only about two hundred miles from Toronto, and on the same latitude as northern California. Abe Lincoln's son Robert liked the place so much that, in 1883, he and his pal General Philip Sheridan built a private fishing club there. It's still operating.

Here's a recipe for fresh-caught trout.

3 to 4 tbsp. butter	¼ cup almonds, sliced
2 trout, filleted	White Wine Sauce
Salt	(recipe follows)
Freshly ground pepper	

White Wine Sauce

2 tbsp. dry white wine	2 tbsp. whipping
¼ cup fish stock, or	(35%) cream
2 tbsp. clam juice	⅛ tsp. tomato paste
mixed with 2 tbsp.	
water	

In a skillet large enough to hold the fillets, melt butter till foaming. Add trout. Sauté about 3 minutes on each side. Once cooked, sprinkle fish with salt and pepper, remove from skillet, and keep warm on a serving platter.

Add nuts to the unwashed pan and shake. When nuts are toasted, toss over the trout fillets. Do not wash the pan just yet.

To make sauce, pour wine into the fish-frying pan. Add stock and cream. Boil down rapidly, then stir in tomato paste. Continue cooking until sauce is reduced and slightly thickened. Spoon sauce over the fillets and serve.

Serves 2 to 4, depending on size of trout.

Pheasant with Green Apples

According to Greek legend, after capturing the golden fleece, Jason and the Argonauts sailed down the Phasis, and, on their journey home to Greece, discovered the ring-neck pheasant. George Washington imported pheasants from Europe in 1789 to stock his estate, and by 1880 this noble bird with good looks and delicious taste was a common sight on North American tables. Time was that there was a four- to twelve-day hanging period for pheasants, during which the bird partially decomposed and acquired a gamey taste. Now out of fashion, the current practice is to serve pheasant within 48 hours. The best season for pheasant is November to January.

2 tbsp. butter
2 tbsp. corn oil
¼ lb. unsmoked bacon, diced
½ Spanish onion, finely chopped
1 clove garlic, finely chopped
1 pheasant

4 small Granny Smith apples, peeled, cored, and quartered
4 tbsp. apple brandy
1 cup whipping (35%) cream
Salt
Freshly ground black pepper

In an ovenproof casserole, melt butter and corn oil. Add bacon, onion, and garlic and sauté until golden. Remove bacon, onion, and garlic with a slotted spoon; reserve. In remaining fats, brown pheasant on all sides. Remove pheasant and reserve. Pour excess fat from casserole, leaving 1 tablespoon.

Add apples to casserole and sauté until they start to turn golden. Place apples in a bowl. Pour apple brandy over them and set aside.

Return pheasant to casserole; surround with apple slices and brandy, bacon bits, onion, and garlic. Cover and cook on low heat for 10 minutes. Stir in the cream; add salt and freshly ground black pepper to taste. Cover and bake in a 275°F oven for 30 to 45 minutes, or until tender.

To serve, cut pheasant in quarters with kitchen shears. Arrange pieces on a plate surrounded by apple slices. Pour sauce on top. Serve either one-half or one-quarter of the bird to each person, depending on size of bird.

Serves 2 to 4.

Fried Catfish in Beer Batter

Hate to scale fish? Catfish have no scales and few bones, and their taste is sweet. This recipe is suitable for finely grained Great Lakes catfish; it brings out the best flavour of these be-whiskered, stout fish.

¼ cup all-purpose flour	1 bottle beer
2 cups cornmeal	6 catfish fillets
½ tsp. dill weed or tarragon	Flour for coating
1 tbsp. salt	2 tsp. salt
1 tbsp. paprika	¼ tsp. pepper
1 egg	Vegetable oil for frying

In a bowl, mix flour, cornmeal, dill or tarragon, salt, and paprika. In another bowl, stir egg into beer. Add beer mixture to dry ingredients and beat until well combined.

Lightly coat fillets with flour and season with salt and pepper. Dip fillets into cornmeal batter.

In a frying pan, heat one-quarter inch oil until medium hot. (Cornmeal burns quickly.) Place fish in the pan in a single layer. When fish is brown on one side, turn carefully.

Remaining batter can be dropped by tablespoons into hot fat to make tasty fritters.

Serves 3 to 4.

Corn and Cheese Chowder

A huge sandspit, the Eau, protects diked marshes burgeoning with a gorgeous variety of vegetables. Farther east along the Erie shore, cherries and peaches can be found in abundance, and in Kent County, as far as the eye can see, there's corn.

How many ears make up twelve tons of corn? Find out at the Tecumseh corn festival, held annually in late August, because that's how many of those butter-dipped golden cobs are consumed there every year. A favourite method of preparing corn is to soak the ears in their husks in water for an hour, then place them on the barbecue. As the husks blacken, give each a quarter turn. When husks are black all around, the corn is done. Peel off the husks, then salt, pepper, and butter the cobs, and enjoy.

2 cups water
1 large potato, peeled
    and diced
2 bay leaves
½ tsp. ground cumin
1 tsp. salt
½ tsp. sage
3 tbsp. butter
1 medium onion,
    peeled and
    chopped
3 tbsp. all-purpose
    flour
1½ cups whipping
    (35%) cream

1¼ cups kernel corn,
    fresh, canned,
    or frozen
3 tbsp. chopped
    green onion
⅓ cup finely
    chopped parsley
Pinch grated nutmeg
Salt
Pepper
1½ cups grated
    Gouda cheese
1 cup dry white wine

In a large saucepan, bring water to a boil. Add potato, bay leaves, cumin, salt, and sage; if you are using fresh or frozen corn, add corn. Cook for 10 minutes.

While potato is cooking, melt butter in a saucepan and slowly cook onion until it is soft but not brown. Stir in flour and cook for 2 to 3 minutes. Slowly add cream. Stirring constantly, cook over low heat until mixture is thick and smooth. Remove from heat.

If you are using canned corn, add corn to the potato and spices. Remove bay leaves. Stir cream mixture into potato mixture; add green onion, parsley, and nutmeg. Add salt and pepper to taste. Simmer, covered, for 10 minutes.

Turn heat to low and slowly start stirring in the grated cheese. Keep stirring until cheese is melted, then stir in the wine. (Do not allow it to boil.) Serve immediately.

Serves 8.

Chilled Cherry-Plum Soup

"Soup of the evening, beautiful soup," sang the Mock Turtle in *Alice in Wonderland*. And this rich, pink, chilled summer soup is a beautiful start to any meal. A burst of colour.

1 ½ lbs. red or purple plums
1 lb. sweet cherries
¼ tsp. salt
¼ tsp. ground ginger
½ tsp. Dijon mustard

⅓ cup dry red wine
2 tbsp. honey
1 ½ cups buttermilk
Sprig of mint or slice of kiwi

Remove the pits from plums and cherries and chop fruit coarsely. Place fruit and salt in a heavy saucepan and cook, covered, over low heat for 7 to 10 minutes, or until there is liquid and fruit is tender. Add ginger, mustard, wine, and honey. Cover and cook over low heat for 5 more minutes.

Remove from heat and let cool to room temperature. Place two-thirds of the mixture in a blender and purée. Place remaining third in a large bowl. Stir in puréed mixture.

Stir in buttermilk and chill for several hours, until mixture is very cold. Serve garnished with a sprig of mint or a slice of kiwi fruit.

Serves 4.

Savoury Vegetable Cheesecake

Its mother is quiche, its father is cheesecake. The offspring is a velvety-textured luncheon dish, and does them both proud.

3 cups packed coarsely
   grated zucchini
Salt
1 cup minced onion
3 tbsp. butter
½ tsp. salt
2 to 3 cloves garlic,
   crushed
1 cup grated carrot
3 tbsp. all-purpose
   flour
½ tsp. basil
½ tsp. oregano
¼ cup packed parsley,
   freshly minced

1 tbsp. fresh lemon
   juice
3 cups ricotta cheese,
   drained
1 cup packed grated
   mozzarella cheese
½ cup freshly grated
   Parmesan cheese
4 large eggs at room
   temperature
Freshly ground black
   pepper
¼ cup breadcrumbs

Set the grated zucchini in a colander over the sink. Salt lightly and let stand for 15 minutes. Squeeze out all excess moisture.

Sauté the onions in butter with ½ tsp. salt till soft and golden. Add garlic, carrot, zucchini, flour, basil, and oregano. Keep stirring and cook over medium heat for 8 to 10 minutes, or until flour is cooked. Remove from heat; stir in parsley and lemon juice.

In the large bowl of an electric mixer, beat together cheeses and eggs till very light and fluffy. Fold in the sautéed vegetables, then mix well. Season to taste with freshly ground black pepper.

Sprinkle the bottom of a well-buttered 10-inch spring-form pan with breadcrumbs. Turn vegetable-cheese mixture into pan. Bake uncovered in a 375°F oven for 30 minutes. Reduce heat to 350°F and bake another 30 minutes. Turn off the oven, open the door, and leave the cake for 15 additional minutes. Remove from oven and cool for 10 to 15 minutes before cutting and serving. Do not refrigerate until completely cool.

Makes one 10-inch cake.

Southern Fried Chicken

When slavery was declared illegal in the British Empire, black slaves began to escape from the United States to Canada. More followed on what became known as the Underground Railway, and many of them settled in Chatham, Shrewsbury, and Dresden. In 1850, about five thousand took the "railroad to freedom." Uncle Tom's cabin, made famous in the novel by Harriet Beecher Stowe, still stands in Dresden.

And in Shrewsbury, they've been making authentic southern fried chicken for years.

3 2½ to 3 lb. frying chickens, cut into serving pieces	**1½ cups all-purpose flour**
	1½ cups finely ground cornmeal
3 cups evaporated milk	**1½ tsp. salt**
2 eggs	**½ tsp. freshly ground pepper**
2 tbsp. Worcestershire sauce	**4 cups vegetable oil**
Flour for dusting	

Place chicken pieces in a shallow bowl. In another bowl, combine milk, eggs, and Worcestershire sauce. Pour milk mixture over chicken. Cover and refrigerate for about 8 hours, or overnight, turning once.

Remove chicken. (Reserve liquid.) Pat chicken dry with paper towels. Dust with flour. In a large plastic bag mix flour, cornmeal, salt, and pepper. Dip chicken in reserved egg mixture, then drop pieces into plastic bag in batches and shake to coat. Remove from bag, shaking off excess cornmeal. Refrigerate for 30 minutes.

In a wok, deep-fryer, or skillet, heat oil to 365°F. Add chicken a few pieces at a time—do not crowd pan—and fry, turning to brown evenly, for 15 to 20 minutes. (The oil should always be between 350°F and 375°F.)

When chicken is cooked, drain on paper towels and serve hot. To serve cold, cool chicken to room temperature, then transfer to a large container with tight-fitting lid. Refrigerate until cold, then serve. (Chicken can be stored in refrigerator for up to 2 days.)

Serves 10 to 12.

Chicken in a Salt Crust

For a new twist in preparing chicken, pass the salt! *National Geographic* magazine says that Goderich is blessed with one of the ten most beautiful sunsets in the world. The town is also the home of Sifto, the salt company. Pick up a few bags of white stuff when you visit this pretty town.

1 3½ lb. chicken
1 tsp. freshly ground
 pepper
2 sprigs fresh tarragon
3 cups coarse pickling
 salt

3 cups all-purpose flour
1¼ cups water
1 egg, lightly beaten
Mustard Sauce
 (recipe follows)

Sprinkle chicken cavity with pepper. Place tarragon sprigs under skin of chicken breasts, being careful not to tear the skin. Tie feet securely together with kitchen twine. Fold wings and tuck under back of the chicken.

In a large mixing bowl, combine pickling salt, flour, and water to make a stiff dough. Form five-eighths of the dough into a ball; form remaining three-eighths into a smaller ball.

Roll out smaller ball of dough until it is one-half inch thick. It should be slightly larger than chicken. Place the dough in a greased shallow baking pan; set chicken on dough, breast-side up. Roll out larger piece of dough until it is one-half inch thick and lay over chicken. Pinch the two pieces of dough together and seal with water. Make sure that no air can escape and that there are no weaknesses in the crust. Brush top crust lightly with beaten egg. Bake, uncovered, in a 350°F oven for about 2 hours, or until crust is golden brown.

Remove chicken from oven and place on a serving platter. Cover with a cloth napkin and crack crust with a mallet. Cut the chicken in quarters with kitchen shears or a sharp knife. Pour the mustard sauce onto the platter and place chicken pieces on the sauce. Serve extra sauce on the side. (The crust should not be eaten.)

Serves 4.

Mustard Sauce

1 tsp. Dijon mustard
1 tsp. minced fresh
   tarragon
1 tbsp. wine vinegar
1 egg yolk

Pinch salt
½ tsp. freshly ground
   pepper
1 cup safflower or
   peanut oil

Combine all ingredients except oil and whisk well. Add oil in a thin stream and continue whisking until sauce thickens slightly.

Serves 4.

Canada Goose Supreme

On their way south, wild geese stop at Jack Miner's Bird Sanctuary in Kingsville. A half-hour drive from Detroit, the sanctuary is in the migration path of the noble Canada goose.

1 6 to 8 lb. Canada goose
Juice of 1 lemon
1 tsp. salt
¼ tsp. pepper
1 large onion, chopped
1 tart apple, chopped
1 cup chopped celery
1 tbsp. flour
1 tsp. salt
1 tsp. sage
1 tsp. paprika
1 tsp. pepper
8 slices bacon
1 cup apple juice
1 cup grapefruit juice
½ cup prune juice

Stuffing

¼ cup butter
¼ cup chopped onion
1 cup chopped sour or tart apple
1 cup chopped dried apricots
3 cups soft breadcrumbs
1 tsp. salt
⅛ tsp. pepper

Clean goose and remove any pinfeathers. Wash goose thoroughly inside and out and pat dry. Sprinkle goose inside and out with lemon juice, 1 tsp. salt, and pepper.

In a bowl, mix together chopped onion, apple, and celery. Stuff mixture into goose cavity. Place goose in roasting pan. Cover and let stand overnight in a cool place.

To make stuffing: Melt butter in a large saucepan. Add onion and simmer until tender. Stir in apple, apricots, breadcrumbs, salt, and pepper.

Remove vegetables and apple from goose and discard. Fill goose cavity with stuffing. Sew up bird. Mix together flour, 1 tsp. salt, sage, paprika, and pepper, and rub mixture into skin of bird.

Cover the breast of the goose with bacon slices. Mix together apple juice, grapefruit juice, and prune juice. Use this liquid to baste the goose. Roast goose, uncovered, in a 400°F oven for 30 minutes, or until goose is light brown, basting every 15 minutes. Reduce heat to 325°F and bake for another 2½ to 3 hours, or until drumstick wiggles easily.

Ten minutes before the goose is done, remove the bacon slices to allow the breast to brown.

Serves 6.

Tomato Gin Soup

"Versatility" is the middle name of this juicy vegetable (or is it a fruit?). Seasoned with gin, this soup gains a romantic edge and makes a sophisticatd opener to a meal.

5 fresh tomatoes, peeled, seeded, and mashed	½ lb. fresh mushrooms
	3 tbsp. butter
3 garlic cloves, mashed	⅓ cup dry gin
2 cups beef stock	½ tsp. Tabasco
1 tsp. dried thyme	2 cups whipping
½ tsp. salt	(35%) cream
¼ tsp. freshly ground pepper	

In a bowl, combine tomatoes, garlic, beef stock, thyme, salt, and pepper. Mix well.

In a soup pot, sauté the mushrooms in butter for 3 to 4 minutes. Add the tomato mixture, gin, and Tabasco and heat just until liquid begins to boil. Add cream just before serving and heat until liquid is near the boiling point, but do not boil. Serve immediately.

Serves 6.

Roast Turkey with Savoury Sauerkraut

Turkey, a Canadian native, was not given due respect until 1800, when Brillat-Savarin, the French gastronome, tasted it in France and remarked that the turkey "is certainly one of the finest gifts made by the new world to the old." Strathroy has chosen to celebrate our favourite fowl with an annual turkey festival which features turkey treats to eat and amusing turkey races.

8 cups sauerkraut	1 tbsp. paprika
3 cups chopped onions	½ cup margarine
1 cup vegetable oil	1 tsp. salt
½ cup chopped parsley	Freshly ground pepper
2 garlic cloves, minced	1 cup chicken broth
1 tsp. dried red-chili- pepper flakes (no seeds)	1 5½ to 6 lb. half turkey

Place the sauerkraut in a colander and rinse well with cold water. Squeeze dry and set aside. In a very large skillet, sauté the onions in ½ cup of the vegetable oil until they are soft but not brown. Add the parsley, garlic, chili flakes, paprika, and margarine; stir over medium heat until the margarine is melted. Add the sauerkraut to the skillet a handful at a time, stirring thoroughly each time. Add the remaining ½ cup oil a few tablespoons at a time, and sauté until the sauerkraut is golden. Add the salt, pepper, and chicken broth. Transfer the contents of the skillet to a roasting pan just large enough to hold the turkey comfortably. Set the turkey on the sauerkraut cut-side down. Cover.

Bake turkey in a 350°F oven, for 2 hours, or until tender, basting every 30 minutes with pan juices. Add more hot chicken broth, if necessary, to provide liquid for basting and to prevent drying of the sauerkraut. If turkey is not brown enough, uncover, turn oven to 400°F, and brown for 10 minutes.

Arrange the sauerkraut on a heated serving platter. Set the turkey half on the bed of sauerkraut cut-side down. Serve each person some sliced turkey over a spoonful of sauerkraut.

Serves 8.

Cheddar-Monkey Bread

Turophiles became over-zealous in 1866 and produced "The Big Cheese," a 7,300-pound block of "milk's leap to immortality," which went on display at the World's Fair in England. The tangy Cheddar from Ingersoll and surrounding areas has enough culinary uses for anybody to monkey around with.

6 tsp. sugar	3½ to 4 cups all-purpose
½ cup warm water	flour
1 package yeast	1½ cups shredded old
1 cup milk	Cheddar cheese
2 tbsp. butter, melted	Melted butter for
1½ tsp. salt	dipping

In a large bowl, dissolve 2 tsp. of the sugar in warm water. Stir in yeast; let stand for 10 minutes. Add milk, butter, remaining 4 tsp. sugar, and salt. Stir in about 3 cups of the flour to make a stiff dough.

Turn out onto a floured surface and knead until dough is elastic, working in additional flour. (This will take about 8 minutes.) Place dough in a buttered bowl, turning once to butter the top. Cover and let rise in a warm place until doubled in bulk, about 1 hour.

Punch dough down. Turn out onto a lightly floured board and roll out to form a 14 by 12-inch rectangle. Sprinkle cheese over surface of dough. Roll up jelly-roll style starting at long side; cut roll into 1-inch slices. Cut each slice into four pieces. Roll each quarter slice into a ball. Dip each ball in melted butter. Line two 8½ by 4½-inch loaf pans with foil; grease the foil, then layer balls of dough evenly in pans.

Cover pans with a light towel and let dough rise in a warm place for about 1 hour, or until doubled in bulk. Bake in a 375°F oven for 25 to 30 minutes, or until loaves are lightly browned. Remove from pans and cool on racks.

Makes 2 loaves.

Cheddar and Ale Soufflé

You can watch cheese being made from the observation gallery of the Pine River Cheese Factory, in Ripley. They've been at it since 1885 and are not averse to giving visitors a taste. This old-English recipe is a delicious way to eat your cheese.

1 ¼ cups milk
2 tbsp. finely chopped onion
¾ cup ale
1 tsp. salt
½ tsp. dry mustard
⅛ tsp. Tabasco
3 cups grated Cheddar cheese

3 cups cubed bread slices (about 6 to 8 slices of bread)
4 eggs, separated
2 tbsp. melted butter
1 tbsp. caraway seeds

In a saucepan, combine milk and onion; heat to scalding. Add ale, salt, dry mustard, Tabasco, grated cheese, and 2 cups of the bread cubes. In a bowl, beat egg yolks until thick and lemon-coloured; stir into saucepan. In another bowl, beat egg whites until stiff but not dry; fold into mixture in saucepan.

Turn batter into a greased 1 ½-quart casserole. Toss remaining 1 cup bread cubes with melted butter and caraway seeds and sprinkle over top of casserole. Set in a pan filled with hot water to 1 inch from top of casserole. Bake, uncovered, in a 325°F oven for 1 hour and 15 minutes, or until soufflé is delicately brown and firm. A knife inserted in centre should come out clean. Serve at once.

Serves 8.

Old-Fashioned Baked Beans

When the population of a town is 795, they've got to do something unique to be noticed, and the townspeople of Zurich have done just that. The entire village becomes a mall at the end of August. The feature attraction – a baked-beans festival. A slow oven and a long baking time will cook the indigestibility right out of these little legumes.

1 lb. navy beans	1 tbsp. dry mustard
1 ¼ lb. slab smoked bacon, cut into bite-sized chunks	1 tbsp. sweet pickle juice or white vinegar
6 medium onions, minced	¼ cup dark molasses
1 tsp. salt	1 cup brown sugar
1 tsp. pepper	¼ cup ketchup or tomato paste
½ tsp. powdered cloves	¼ tsp. cayenne pepper (optional)
½ tsp. cinnamon	

Place beans in a large container. Cover with water and soak overnight. In the morning, drain the beans and place them in a large pot. Cover with cold water until pot is three-quarters full. Add all remaining ingredients.

Bring to boil, then turn heat to medium. Simmer for 1 hour. Cover and transfer to oven. Bake in a 275°F oven for about 6 to 8 hours, or until moisture evaporates, stirring about once an hour. For browner beans, uncover for the last hour.

Serves 8.

Chili Sauce

"Love apples" or, as we call them, tomatoes were gathered wild in their native Peru. Then the tomato made its saucy way, via Morocco where it was dubbed *pomi di mori*, to Italy, where it is called *Pomodoro*, and France, where it is *Pomme d'amour*. Europeans believed it was poisonous (the leaves *are* toxic) and used it as decorative foliage for arbours and outhouses. But we know exactly what to do with this tender succulent.

4 cinnamon sticks, broken in pieces	**15 choice dead-ripe tomatoes (about 4 lbs.)**
10 whole cloves	**3 sweet red peppers**
1 tbsp. celery seed	**1 sweet green pepper**
6 whole black peppercorns	**3 large onions**
3 or 4 small red chilies	**4 tsp. coarse salt**
3 cups cider vinegar	**1½ cups sugar**

Place broken cinnamon sticks, cloves, celery seed, peppercorns, and chilies in a cheesecloth bag. Pour vinegar into a large pot. Add spice bag and bring vinegar to a boil. Let simmer covered for 20 minutes. Lift out spice bag and squeeze well into the vinegar.

Peel tomatoes and cut into small pieces. Wash red and green peppers, cut in half and remove seeds. Finely chop onions and peppers by hand or in a food chopper, taking care not to purée or liquefy them. Add tomatoes, peppers, and onions to vinegar mixture. Add salt and ½ cup of the sugar.

Simmer over low heat for 30 minutes. Then add remaining 1 cup of sugar and boil rapidly, stirring often, until sauce thickens.

Makes about 8 cups.

Eggplant and Cracked-Wheat Casserole

An unusual blend of ingredients gives this Mediterranean casserole an intriguing aroma and taste.

**2 large cloves garlic,
  crushed
1 cup chopped onion
3 tbsp. olive oil
½ lb. mushrooms,
  chopped
1 ½ lb. eggplant,
  cut in 1-inch
  cubes
½ tsp. dill
½ tsp. ground cumin
1 tsp. salt
Pinch cayenne
  pepper**

**Juice from 1 medium
  lemon
½ cup currants
½ cup raw cracked
  wheat
1 tsp. honey
2 tbsp. butter
2 tbsp. all-purpose
  flour
1 ¾ cups hot milk
2 hard-boiled eggs,
  grated
Pinch paprika**

In a large frying pan, sauté the garlic and onions in olive oil over moderate heat, 3 to 4 minutes, till onion is soft and golden. Stir in the mushrooms, eggplant, dill, cumin, salt, cayenne, and lemon juice. Cook, stirring, over medium heat for 5 to 8 minutes, until lightly browned.

Add currants, cracked wheat, and honey. Stir well and cover. Simmer over medium-low heat for about 12 minutes, stirring occasionally. When the eggplant is tender, remove the pan from heat and spread mixture into a greased 9 by 13-inch baking pan.

In a small saucepan, melt butter over low heat. Sprinkle in flour and cook for 3 to 4 minutes, stirring constantly. Pour in hot milk all at once and whisk till smooth and thick, about 5 minutes. Remove from heat and stir in the grated eggs.

Pour sauce over the eggplant mixture and spread as evenly as possible. Dust the top with paprika and bake, uncovered, in a 350°F oven for 30 minutes, or until top is light brown.

Serves 6.

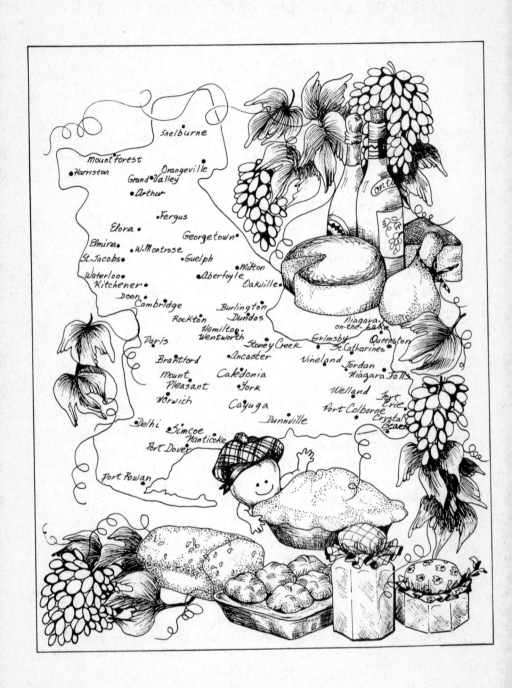

CHAPTER 2

FESTIVALS OF ORCHARDS,VINEYARDS, AND HARVEST

*Spectacular Niagara Falls thunders
at the heart of this colourful region. Lesser
waterfalls and streams are punctuated by old mills,
once the hub of the area's industry. Today, many have
been restored as charming inns and fine restaurants.
English, Scottish, Mennonites, and Germans, among
others, joined the original native settlers here. Their
traditions, which enhance the quality of our life, are kept
alive with festivals of sport, food, wine, and theatre.*

Recipes

Restaurants of the Region

ALTON

The Millcroft Inn • An elegant country hotel with a glass dining pod that hangs right over the rushing water and adds a special excitement to one of the area's most brilliant dining rooms. The huge terrace is like a stone dock built right over the water

ANCASTER

Ancaster Old Mill • A sun-dappled, glass-walled dining room overlooking a splashing mill stream, with excellent fare, in a mill built in the early 1800s

BRANTFORD

Heritage Inn • An 1840 octagonal house – Fine dining

The Olde School Restaurant • A reconstructed 1870s school house. Try the house specialties

CAMBRIDGE

The Mill at Cambridge • The mill shows off its river dam and falls by seating diners in a glassed-in terrace overlooking nature's beauty. Filet mignon, rack of lamb, and whole fresh trout are featured

CONESTOGA

Black Forest Inn • Enjoy schnitzel, ribs, and rouladen in Bavarian-style inn

DUNNVILLE

The Hartford • Traditional British fare with English ale and beer

ELORA

The Desert Rose Café • Tiny vegetarian and Mexican café

The Elora Mill Inn • The walls of the mill rise dramatically from the very edge of the rushing Grand River. The windows of the dining room look out on a view of the Tooth of Time, a narrow jut of rock that divides the river as it plunges into the Elora gorge. A ruggedly romantic dining room and selection of antique furnished rooms

FORT ERIE

Herbert's • In summer sit at tables on the lawn overlooking the Niagara River and enjoy European cooking

GUELPH

Baker Street Bistro • Quiet intimate dining room, large portions, and artwork on the walls

The Bookshelf Café • Half bookstore, half restaurant, with an interesting menu

KITCHENER-WATERLOO

The Brittany • French fare

The Cedars of Lebanon • Entertainment on week-ends, authentic and exciting Middle Eastern food

The Charcoal Steak House • Steaks, ribs, and Mennonite pig tails

Linwood Tavern • Charming country pub with homey atmosphere

Olde Heidelberg House • In the heart of Mennonite country, features farmers' sausages, ribs and kraut

NEW HAMBURG

The Waterlot Inn • Charming French cuisine

NIAGARA-ON-THE-LAKE

Oban Inn • Large, white buildings with lovely gardens and a view of the lake. An English/Canadian menu

The Pillar & Post Restaurant • Light lunches and traditional dinners

Prince of Wales Hotel • The Prince of Wales Hotel was host to royalty as far back as 1901. During the Shaw Festival season this large formal dining room becomes very busy, but with no drop in the quality of food and service

NIAGARA FALLS

Reese's • Formal dining room

NORMANDALE

Union Hotel • Simple fresh food

PETERSBURG

The Blue Moon • Entertainment, sing-alongs. Specialties are pig-tails and pork hocks

PORT DALHOUSIE

Maria's • Wonderful lobster dinners in a noisy and friendly atmosphere

PORT DOVER

Erie Beach Hotel • A huge ramshackle building dominating the crescent-shaped beach at Port Dover on Lake Erie. The kind of casual yet dignified spot you hope for in a pretty fishing hamlet

Fred Knechtel Foods • Great fish and chips

ROCKWOOD

La Vieille Auberge • An old stone building with a tempting French menu

ST. JACOBS

Jacobstettel Guest House • Where time stands still and the most exciting event occurs when the apple cake with hot butter sauce or the chocolate chip cookies come out of the oven and guests help themselves in the kitchen

ST. MARY'S

The Contented Mouse • Fresh herbs, rich cream, baking, and absolutely delicious light meals

Baked Indian Pudding

"Brantford Binder Twine" were the first words I learned to read. They were on a large picture calendar that hung over my bed at our family farm, where the battery-powered radio was turned on only for the nine-o'clock news, where television was still science fiction, and where the only book I saw was the alphabet book my older sister brought home from school. That calendar was a wonderful game of letters and numbers to me. I imagined Brantford was some special, beautiful, faraway place.

Decades later, I found that it was indeed a special, beautiful place. I learned that during the American Revolution, the Six Nations – Oneida, Cayuga, Onondaga, Seneca, Tuscarora, and Mohawk Indians – fought for the British, led by Chief Joseph Brant. They were given seven hundred thousand acres of land on the beautiful Grand River, and, in 1784, Brant led them to the first Indian reserve in Canada. Brant was decorated by King George III, and the church the Six Nations built became the Royal Chapel of the Mohawks.

Corn was their staff of life.

4 cups whole milk	2 tbsp. butter
½ tsp. salt	1 cup milk, room
⅓ cup molasses	temperature
1 tsp. ground	Whipped cream for
ginger	garnish
⅓ cup sugar	Chopped preserved
½ cup cornmeal	ginger for garnish

In the top of a double boiler over boiling water, heat milk until bubbles form around the edge of the pan. Stir in salt, molasses, ground ginger, and sugar; gradually stir in cornmeal. Cook, stirring constantly, until mixture has thickened. Remove from heat and stir in butter, then pour into a buttered 2-quart baking dish. Set the baking dish in a large pan and fill the pan with boiling water to two-thirds the depth of the baking dish. Bake, uncovered, in a 400°F oven. After 45 minutes, stir in the warm milk; continue to bake for 45 minutes more.

Serve warm or cold. The pudding is good topped with whipped cream and sprinkled with chopped preserved ginger.

Serves 6.

Native Canadian Squash Soup

A thick yet light soup that needs no cream.

¼ cup corn oil or
    butter
2 carrots, peeled and
    sliced
1 leek, cleaned and
    sliced
2 lbs. butternut
    squash, fresh or
    frozen, diced
7 cups chicken broth

1 bay leaf
3 peppercorns, crushed
Salt
Pepper
½ cup diced yellow
    squash
½ cup seeded diced
    cucumber
2 tbsp. honey

In a thick-bottomed pot, heat oil or butter. Sauté carrots, leek, and butternut squash until soft. Add chicken broth, bay leaf, and peppercorns and bring to a boil—this should take about 10 minutes – stirring constantly to avoid sticking.

Force soup through a coarse strainer. (For very smooth soup, pour into blender and purée.) Salt and pepper to taste.

Blanch yellow squash and cucumber in hot water until tender, about 3 minutes. Drain and set squash and cucumber in individual soup bowls.

Add honey to soup, stir, and pour soup over vegetables. Serve hot.

Serves 8.

Fettuccine with Chèvre and Herbs

After a lush summer lunch at a country inn in the south of France, the waiter brought the cheese course: a napkin-lined wicker tray filled with little cubes, small circles wrapped in chestnut and grape leaves, chalky white logs, and flat-topped pyramids dusted with wood ash. It was my first taste of chèvre, the creamy cheese made from goat's milk.

In Elmira, I discovered Woolwich's Dairy, which manufactures several varieties of chèvre – cream, feta, tarragon, and farmhouse. Low in calories and butterfat, they're great for dieters, and a treat for those allergic to cow's milk.

*1¼ cups whipping
(35%) cream
¼ cup milk
¼ tsp. minced garlic
6 oz. chèvre, rind
removed, cut into
1-inch cubes
1 tsp. white wine
vinegar*

*Coarse salt
Freshly ground pepper
1 lb. fresh fettuccine
4 tbsp. chopped fresh
herbs (basil,
Italian parsley,
or rosemary)
or 2 tbsp.
dried herbs*

In a heavy, medium-size saucepan, heat cream, milk, and garlic over low heat until bubbles form around edges of liquid. Remove from heat; add chèvre cubes and whisk until cheese is melted and mixture is smooth. Add vinegar; add salt and pepper to taste. Let sauce stand, covered, for 15 minutes.

Meanwhile, in a large kettle, bring salted water to a boil. Add fettuccine; cook until tender but firm, 1 to 3 minutes. Drain in a large colander; transfer to warmed platter.

Return sauce to low heat and stir in herbs. Pour over pasta and toss thoroughly. Grind pepper over pasta. Serve immediately.

Makes 8 first-course servings, or 4 to 6 main-course servings.

Chèvre Coeur à la Crème

Light and lush, this dish is a simple, perfect accompaniment to summer berries.

8 oz. chèvre
⅔ cup cottage cheese
6 tbsp. whipping (35%)
cream
1 tbsp. plus 2 tsp.
sugar

Fresh strawberries
or raspberries,
rinsed, patted
dry, and hulled

Line a 2-cup *coeur à la crème* mould (see Note) with a double thickness of cheesecloth, allowing the cloth to hang over the sides; rest mould on rim of shallow pan or bowl. (The bowl will collect draining liquid.)

In the bowl of an electric mixer, combine chèvre, cottage cheese, whipping cream, and sugar. Beat at low speed until mixture is smooth. Spoon cheese mixture into prepared mould and cover securely with aluminum foil. Place mould, on its shallow pan, in the refrigerator and chill until cheese mixture is firm, about 2 days.

Discard liquid in pan. Invert mould onto a serving plate, surround with berries, and serve.

Serves 6 to 8.

Note: A 2-cup aluminum-foil baking pan with pinholes punched at 1-inch intervals can also be used.

Peanut-Butter Pie with Chocolate Crust

Peanuts grow in northern New Mexico, so why not in southern Ontario? They have a similar climate. The Picard family grows eight hundred thousand pounds of red-skinned Valencia peanuts a year on the shores of Lake Erie, just southwest of Brantford.

Crust

30 *plain chocolate wafer biscuits*

7 *tbsp. unsalted butter, melted*

Filling

1 *quart vanilla ice cream, slightly softened*
¾ *cup creamy peanut butter*

1 *cup unsalted peanuts, chopped*
1 *tbsp. vanilla*
1 *cup whipping (35%) cream*
Hot-Fudge Sauce (recipe follows)

To make crust: Put wafers in a plastic bag and crush to very fine crumbs with a rolling pin, or pulverize wafers in a food processor. You should have about 1½ cups of crumbs. Add melted butter and mix well.

Press mixture evenly over the bottom and sides of a deep 9-inch pie plate. Bake in a 300°F oven for 10 minutes. Cool to room temperature before filling.

To make filling: Combine ice cream, peanut butter, ½ cup of the nuts, and vanilla in a bowl. Mix well. Pour into crust, sprinkle with remaining nuts, and place in freezer for 6 hours or overnight, until pie is frozen and firm.

Remove 10 minutes before serving. Whip cream until stiff. Garnish pie with drizzled Hot-Fudge Sauce and whipped cream.

Makes one 9-inch pie.

Hot-Fudge Sauce

½ cup cocoa
¾ cup sugar
⅔ cup evaporated
milk

⅓ cup light corn
syrup
⅓ cup butter or
margarine
1 tsp. vanilla

In a saucepan, combine cocoa and sugar. Stir in evaporated milk and corn syrup. Cook over medium heat, stirring constantly, until mixture boils; boil and stir for 1 minute.

Remove from heat; stir in butter or margarine and vanilla. Serve hot.

Makes about 1½ cups.

Shoo-Fly Pie

Put this pie on the window to cool, and its sticky sweetness will have you constantly saying, "Shoo, fly."

½ tsp. baking soda
¾ cup boiling water
1 cup dark mild
molasses
½ cup brown sugar

1½ cups all-purpose
flour
¼ cup shortening
1 9-inch pie crust
(see p. 95)

In a small bowl, dissolve baking soda in boiling water. Add molasses and stir.

In another bowl, combine brown sugar and flour. Using your fingers, rub in shortening until mixture forms into crumbs.

Pour one-third of the molasses mixture into unbaked pie crust; then add one-third of the crumb mixture. Continue to make layers, ending up with crumbs. Bake in a 375°F oven for approximately 35 minutes, or until crust and crumb mixture are brown.

Makes one 9-inch pie.

Paper-Bag Purple-Plum Pie

This pie, made from summer-ripe plums can light up your dessert table and leave your oven spotless.

Filling

4 cups fresh purple
    plums, halved and
    pitted
1 tbsp. lemon juice
½ cup sugar

¼ cup all-purpose flour
¼ tsp. salt
¼ tsp. nutmeg
1 9-inch pastry shell,
    unbaked

Topping

½ cup all-purpose flour
½ cup white sugar
½ tsp. cinnamon

½ cup butter or
    margarine

In a large bowl, sprinkle the plums with lemon juice. Add sugar, flour, salt, and nutmeg. Mix well and ladle into uncooked pastry shell.

To make topping: In a bowl, combine flour, sugar, and cinnamon. Cut in the butter. Sprinkle topping over plums.

Place the pie in a heavy brown-paper bag. Fold end of bag twice and fasten with a paper clip. Place on a cookie sheet and set in preheated 425°F oven. Bake for 1 hour. Remove from oven, but do not remove pie from the bag until juice stops bubbling.

Makes one 9-inch pie.

Fabulous Truffles

The name "Laura Secord" is synonymous with the most popular flavour in the world – chocolate. A heroic woman, Laura Secord overheard some American troops planning a surprise attack against the British early on in the War of 1812. She ran through twenty miles of bush and swamp to warn the British, enabling them to gain a decisive victory at the Battle of Beaver Dams. Laura Secord has been honoured by having an entire chocolate collection named after her.

½ cup butter	2 tbsp. liqueur
1 cup cocoa	Icing sugar
¾ cup sugar	Cocoa
½ cup whipping (35%) cream	Chopped toasted nuts

In a saucepan over medium-high heat, melt butter until it bubbles. Remove from heat and blend in cocoa and sugar. Stir in cream and liqueur. Chill until mixture is firm enough to shape. Roll spoonfuls between your hands to form 1-inch balls. Roll each ball in icing sugar, cocoa, or nuts. Store, covered, in refrigerator.

Makes about 2 dozen truffles.

Carrot Bundt Cake

In southwest Ontario, beautiful old mills dot the landscape. Many date back to the eighteen hundreds. The flour produced by the mills makes the area's baking so delicious that everything else is just icing on the cake.

Dark, heavy, and moist, this carrot cake is the best.

1½ cups vegetable oil
2 cups sugar
4 eggs
2 cups all-purpose flour
2 tsp. baking powder
1½ tsp. baking soda
1 tsp. salt

5 tsp. cinnamon
2 cups grated carrots
1 cup crushed
  pineapple, drained
1 cup chopped walnuts
1 tsp. vanilla

Icing

8 oz. (500 g) cream
  cheese
1 cup icing sugar

1 tbsp. orange juice

In the bowl of an electric mixer, combine oil and sugar. Add eggs one at a time and beat after each addition.

In a separate bowl, mix together flour, baking powder, soda, salt, and cinnamon. Add to oil mixture and beat. Stir in grated carrots, pineapple, walnuts, and vanilla.

Pour into a well-greased 12-cup Bundt pan and bake in preheated 350°F oven for 45 minutes to 1 hour, or until toothpick inserted in cake comes out clean. Allow cake to cool before icing.

To make icing: In small bowl of electric mixer, combine cream cheese, icing sugar, and orange juice and beat at low speed until icing is smooth and creamy.

Makes 1 large Bundt cake.

Poppy-Seed Bundt Cake

A cake with a rich, homemade taste and texture.

¼ cup poppy seeds
1 cup buttermilk
1 cup butter or
   margarine
1½ cups sugar
4 egg yolks
1 tsp. vanilla
2½ cups all-purpose flour

1 tsp. baking soda
2 tsp. baking powder
½ tsp. salt
4 egg whites
½ cup tiny chocolate
   chips
3 tsp. cinnamon
4 tsp. sugar

In a small bowl, soak poppy seeds in buttermilk for 20 minutes.

In a large mixing bowl, cream butter and 1½ cups sugar; beat until fluffy. Add egg yolks and vanilla and beat.

In a separate bowl, mix together flour, soda, baking powder, and salt. Add to butter mixture alternately with buttermilk-poppy-seed mixture.

Beat egg whites until stiff and fold into batter; then fold in chocolate chips.

Grease a 12-cup Bundt pan and put in one-third of the batter. In a small bowl, combine cinnamon and 4 tsp. sugar; sprinkle half of it over the batter. Add another third of the batter. Sprinkle with remaining cinnamon-sugar; then add remaining batter. Bake in a preheated 350°F oven for 1 hour, or until toothpick inserted in cake comes out clean.

Makes 1 large Bundt cake.

Chocolate Date Loaf

A moist, dense loaf that goes a long way.

1 cup dates	1 ¾ cups all-purpose flour
1 cup boiling water	½ tsp. salt
1 tsp. baking soda	3 tbsp. cocoa
1 cup vegetable	1 tsp. vanilla
shortening	½ cup chopped nuts
1 cup sugar	½ cup chocolate chips
2 eggs	

Chop the dates. In a mixing bowl, stir together boiling water and baking soda; stir in dates.

In a large bowl, cream shortening and sugar; beat in eggs.

In a separate bowl, mix together flour, salt, and cocoa and add to sugar-and-egg mixture. Add vanilla and dates, with their liquid, and blend well.

Pour batter into two greased 9 by 5-inch loaf pans. Sprinkle batter with chocolate chips and nuts, and pat down lightly. Bake in a preheated 325°F oven for 1 hour, or until toothpick inserted in centre of loaf comes out clean.

Makes 2 loaves.

Rice Muffins

Versatility is the middle name of these muffins: they are good as a side dish for fish, especially salmon patties, with sour cream. Or serve with yogurt and fruit for lunch or tea.

2 cups water	2 eggs, beaten
2 cups milk	1 cup sour cream
1 tsp. salt	¼ tsp. baking soda
1 cup rice	¾ cup all-purpose flour
¼ cup sugar	1 tsp. baking powder
¼ cup butter	

In a large saucepan with a tight-fitting lid, boil the water. Add milk, ½ tsp. of the salt, and the rice. Cook, covered, on low heat until all liquid is absorbed, about 30 minutes. Stir in sugar and butter and let cool. When cool, stir in eggs.

In a bowl, combine sour cream and baking soda. In a separate bowl, mix together flour, baking powder, and remaining ½ tsp. salt. Add sour-cream mixture and flour mixture alternately to rice.

Fill 24 greased muffin cups two-thirds full with batter and bake in a 375°F oven for 45 minutes, or until golden brown. Cool on racks.

Makes 24 muffins.

Pumpkin Bundt Cake

A moist, rich cake with the flavours of autumn.

2 cups all-purpose flour	1 ¾ cups sugar
1 cup natural bran	1 ½ tsp. cinnamon
2 tsp. baking powder	4 eggs
1 tsp. baking soda	1 cup vegetable oil
½ tsp. allspice	1 14-oz. can pumpkin
⅛ tsp. cloves	1 cup chocolate chips
⅛ tsp. ginger	or chopped nuts

In a bowl, combine flour, bran, baking powder, baking soda, allspice, cloves, ginger, sugar, and cinnamon.

In a large mixing bowl, beat eggs and oil together. Beat in pumpkin. Add flour mixture and mix well; then add chocolate chips or nuts.

Pour batter into a greased 12-cup Bundt pan and bake in a 350°F oven for 1 hour, or until toothpick inserted in cake comes out clean.

Makes 1 Bundt cake.

Applesauce Raisin Cake with Lemon Glaze

A family favourite – wonderful for after school.

Cake

1 ¾ cups white sugar
1 cup butter
2 cups unsweetened applesauce
1 tsp. grated lemon rind
1 tsp. vanilla

3 cups all-purpose flour
1 tsp. cinnamon
1 tsp. nutmeg
2 tsp. baking soda
1 cup raisins

Lemon-Cinnamon Glaze

1 cup icing sugar
2 tbsp. lemon juice

½ tsp. grated lemon rind
½ tsp. grated nutmeg

Butter and flour a 10-inch Bundt pan. In a large mixing bowl, beat together sugar and butter until mixture is light in colour. Beat in applesauce, lemon rind, and vanilla. Sprinkle flour, cinnamon, nutmeg, baking soda, and raisins over applesauce mixture and stir just until mixed.

Pour batter into greased and floured pan. Bake in a preheated 325°F oven for 1 hour and 10 minutes, or until a toothpick inserted in cake comes out clean.

Remove cake from oven and let it cool in the pan for 20 minutes, then remove from pan and cool on a rack.

To make glaze: In a small bowl, combine icing sugar, lemon juice, lemon rind, and nutmeg. Stir until well mixed. Spread icing over top of cake and let drizzle down sides.

Makes one 10-inch cake.

Apple Cake

Spy, Empire, Cortland, Ida Red, Melba, Jersymac, Wealthy, Quinte, Lodi, McIntosh, Red, and Golden Delicious: luscious apples are available all year round. Apple trees live a long time. In the early 1900s, the trees grown below the Stoney Creek escarpment by the E. D. Smith nursery were shipped to Nova Scotia to start a fledgling orchard. Do they remember their roots?

2 *eggs, beaten*	1 *tsp. baking soda*
1 *cup sugar*	1 *tsp. cinnamon*
1 *tsp. vanilla*	3 *cups peeled, sliced*
3 *cups all-purpose*	*apples*
flour	1 *cup vegetable oil*
½ *tsp. salt*	½ *cup brown sugar*

In a large bowl, beat together eggs and sugar. Beat in vanilla.

Sift together flour, salt, soda, and cinnamon and add to egg mixture. Stir in apples. Pour in oil and mix well.

Pour batter into a greased 9 by 13-inch pan. Sprinkle with brown sugar. Bake in a 300°F oven for about 1 hour, or until toothpick inserted in centre comes out clean.

This dessert is delicious topped with yogurt mixed with a little cinnamon and grated orange rind.

Makes 1 cake.

Plum Dumplings

A hearty, stick-to-the-ribs, home-style side dish, or a satisfying lunch with sour cream on the side.

12 *purple plums*	1 *egg yolk*
12 *sugar cubes*	½ *cup butter*
Ground cinnamon	*Pinch salt*
6 *potatoes*	1 *cup fine dry*
2 to 3 *cups all-*	*breadcrumbs*
purpose flour	3 *tbsp. butter*

Without completely separating the halves, pit the plums. Roll sugar cubes in cinnamon. Replace each pit with a sugar cube.

Boil potatoes in skins until soft. Peel, mash, and measure quantity. Place potatoes in a large mixing bowl. Add an equal amount of flour, the egg yolk, ½ cup butter, and salt. Turn onto a lightly floured board and knead until dough is no longer sticky. (This will take about 7 minutes.) Roll dough out to a thickness of one-quarter inch. Cut into twelve 4-inch squares and place a plum in the centre of each square. Bring the four corners of each square together to make a round dumpling and seal each dumpling well; dumplings should be watertight.

Into a large kettle of boiling salted water, drop dumplings a few at a time and cook for 15 minutes. If any dumplings stick to the bottom of the pot, prod them gently until they rise to the surface.

While dumplings are cooking, in a skillet, brown breadcrumbs in 3 tbsp. butter and keep warm. Remove dumplings from kettle with a slotted spoon and roll each in breadcrumbs. Serve hot as a side dish with meat or as a luncheon dish with sour cream or yogurt.

Makes 12 dumplings.

Crême Brulée

Dairy land. Placid Holsteins grazing in fields are reminiscent of old calendar pictures. Near the village of St. George stands the home of Adelaide Hunter Hoodless, who crusaded many years ago for the pasteurization of milk. Her work led to the founding of the Women's Institute, an eight-million-strong international organization with branches in the rural areas of most civilized nations. Christina Smith, wife of E.D. Smith (maker of jams, jellies, and pie fillings), was the institute's first president. Besides advocating healthful eating, she led the crusade for shorter skirts in the early 1900s.

4 cups cereal (10%) cream
8 egg yolks
½ cup sugar

1 tsp. vanilla
½ cup brown sugar

In the top of a 2-quart double boiler over hot water, heat cream. In a separate bowl, beat egg yolks until light; then beat in sugar and vanilla. Stir in warm cream. Pour custard into an 8 by 6½ by 1¼-inch baking dish. Place dish in a large pan; fill the pan with boiling water to a depth of one-half inch. Cover baking dish and pan loosely with aluminum foil and place in a 325°F oven. Bake for 30 minutes, or until a toothpick inserted in centre comes out dry. Cool completely, then refrigerate for at least 4 hours.

Sift brown sugar to remove any lumps. Spoon sugar lightly and evenly over custard. Place custard under a preheated broiler. Leave door open and watch the crême carefully: do not allow the brown sugar to scorch. It should just melt. Broil for 3 minutes, or until sugar melts to form a smooth caramel glaze.

Remove from oven and place in the freezer for about 10 minutes until glaze hardens. Crack with a spoon to serve.

Serves 10 to 12.

Rouladen

Kitchener-Waterloo is a centre of German immigration. The cities'
inhabitants take pride in their cultural heritage. The yearly Oktoberfest, redolent with *Gemütlichkeit*, is the largest harvest festival of
its type in North America. Sparkling beer steins abound, along with
mountains of sausage and sauerkraut and lots of traditional favourites, like rouladen, an ordinary round steak that becomes a gourmet delight with the addition of a little ingenuity and a pickle.

**3 lbs. top-of-the-round
  steak**
**2 cups finely chopped
  onion**
5 tbsp. vegetable oil
2 tbsp. hot mustard
Freshly ground pepper
**3 dill pickles, sliced in
  half lengthwise**
**2 medium onions,
  cut into quarters**

**2 ripe tomatoes, cut
  into quarters**
1 cup water
2 tsp. cornstarch
½ cup dry red wine
**½ cup whipping (35%)
  cream**
Salt
Freshly ground pepper

Cut the beef into 6 half-inch-thick pieces. Pound each piece
until it is about one-quarter inch thick and measures 4 by 8
inches.

In a skillet, sauté the onions in 2 tbsp. of the oil until onions
are soft. Remove from heat. Spread each beef slice with a
teaspoon of mustard, then sprinkle with cooked onion.
Grate a little pepper over each slice. Place a slice of pickle
across the bottom of each beef slice and roll up jelly-roll
fashion. Tie each roll securely with string.

In a heavy casserole over medium-high heat, heat remaining
3 tbsp. oil. Place beef rolls in hot oil. When first side is
brown, turn the rolls and add the onion quarters and tomato
pieces. Beef and vegetables should brown; do not let them
burn. When they are brown, pour in the water and stir to
loosen the browned particles from the bottom of the
casserole. Turn heat to low, cover the casserole, and let the
rouladen simmer for about 1 hour and 30 minutes, or until

the meat is just tender. Baste with cooking juices once or twice while simmering to keep beef moist.

Remove rouladen to a platter and keep warm. Strain the cooking liquid, then return it to the casserole and bring to a boil. In a small bowl, mix cornstarch with red wine and whisk into the boiling liquid. Stir until the sauce is thick and smooth.

Stir in cream, add salt and pepper to taste, and pour sauce over rouladen. Serve immediately.

These are good with buttered noodles.

Serves 6.

Sweetbreads in Cream Sauce

A flavourful first course to delight guests.

½ lb. calf sweetbreads
2 tsp. chopped capers
1 tbsp. butter
1 tsp. white wine
1 tsp. brandy
½ cup whipping (35%)
  cream

2 tbsp. cold water
1 tbsp. all-purpose
  flour
Salt
Pepper
1 tbsp. fresh chopped
  parsley

In a large saucepan, sauté sweetbreads and capers in butter for a few minutes, or until sweetbreads are opaque. Add white wine. When liquid is nearly boiling, add brandy. Light brandy and let it flame. When brandy has stopped flaming, stir in cream. Continue cooking, taking care not to let the sauce boil, for about 15 minutes, or until the sweetbreads are tender. In a small bowl, stir together cold water, flour, salt and pepper to taste, and chopped parsley. Add to sauce. Cook, stirring, until sauce thickens, about 3 minutes.

Sweetbreads are delicious with rice – white or wild – and fresh vegetables.

Serves 2.

Roast Suckling Pig

Let's go "whole hog." This traditional feast will turn any occasion into a merry gathering.

4- to 5-week-old pig	**1 cup chicken broth**
(15 to 18 lbs.)	**1 red apple**
Bacon fat	**2 cherries or 2**
Salt	**cranberries**
Pepper	**Parsley**

Stuffing

Liver, heart, and	**Pepper**
kidneys from	**⅓ cup green olives,**
pig	**chopped**
1 lb. fresh pork-	**½ cup sherry**
sausage meat	**1 egg, beaten**
1 large onion, chopped	**1 lb. black walnuts**
5 medium mushrooms,	**1½ to 2 cups coarse**
chopped	**breadcrumbs**
2 cups chicken broth	**1 cup chopped celery**
1 clove garlic,	**1 tbsp. chopped**
minced	**parsley**
Salt	**Dash of brandy**

Marinade

3 cups oil	**½ bay leaf**
½ cup brandy	**1 onion, sliced**
2 carrots, sliced	**1 clove garlic, crushed**
1 tsp. chopped parsley	**Salt**
½ tsp. thyme	**Pepper**

To prepare pig: Have the butcher bone the pig, leaving in leg bones and hooves. Be sure you have the liver, heart, and kidneys.

Wash the pig thoroughly, singe hairs, wash again, and drain well with the head down. Wipe dry, rub with bacon fat inside and out, and sprinkle with salt and pepper.

To make the stuffing: In a saucepan, cover liver, heart, and kidneys with water and simmer until tender, about 40 minutes. Drain and chop fine. In a large skillet over medium heat, sauté the sausage meat, onion, and mushrooms until sausage is done. In a separate pan, bring the chicken broth to a boil. Add the garlic, salt and pepper to taste, olives, and sherry. Simmer for about 5 minutes. Remove from heat, then stir in the chopped liver, heart, and kidney. Stir in the egg and walnuts. Add enough of the breadcrumbs to make a moist dressing. Stir in the celery, parsley, brandy, and salt and pepper to taste.

Stuff the prepared pig, sew up securely, and tie the legs in kneeling position.

To make marinade: In a large bowl, mix all the marinade ingredients. Pour half the marinade in a bowl large enough to accommodate the pig. Add the stuffed pig and pour the rest of the marinade over it. Cover and marinate in the refrigerator for 1 day, turning pig occasionally.

On a rack lined with heavy aluminum foil, place the stuffed, prepared pig in a kneeling position. Set rack in a roasting pan and turn the foil up loosely around the pig. Cover the ears with foil and place a tightly rolled ball of foil in the mouth. Place more foil or wet cooking parchment over the pig. Roast pig in a 350°F oven for about 3 hours, basting first with the chicken broth and then with pan drippings. Replace the covering foil after each basting. (If you are using parchment, wet it after each basting.) About 45 minutes before the pig is done, remove the foil or parchment to let the skin brown.

Place the pig on a hot platter. Replace the ball of foil with a red apple and put cranberries or cherries in for eyes. Garnish with parsley. The pan liquid can be used to make scrapple.

Serves 10 to 12.

Apple Cake with Hot Butter Sauce

Mennonites and Amish lead simple and quiet lives. St. Jacobs is just a few hours from Toronto, but the peace of the community is broken only by the sound of buggy wheels, the cadence of crickets, and the buzz of a hand-pushed lawnmower. Many meals are taken at the community dining hall, where traditional dishes like *Obsttorte* and *snitz and knepp* are served. Once a year, about thirty thousand visitors converge in New Hamburg for a crack-of-dawn pancake-and-sausage breakfast, which opens the Ontario Mennonite Relief Auction, to aid medical, educational, and agricultural projects throughout the world. At the auction you can buy jams, jellies, fruit pies, and household accessories, all lovingly handcrafted by this caring group.

Cake

2½ cups sifted all-purpose flour
2 tsp. baking soda
½ tsp. salt
1 tsp. nutmeg
1 tsp. cinnamon

3½ cups peeled, cored, and diced apples
½ cup soft butter or shortening
1½ cups sugar
2 eggs

Hot Butter Sauce

½ cup butter
1 tbsp. all-purpose flour
½ cup brown sugar

½ cup sugar
½ cup table (18%) cream
1 tsp. rum flavouring

In a large bowl, combine flour, soda, salt, nutmeg, and cinnamon. Add apples. In a separate bowl, cream butter and sugar well; beat in eggs.

Add butter-and-sugar mixture to flour-and-apple mixture, stirring until flour is just moistened; do not overmix. Pour batter into a greased 9-inch square pan and bake in a 350°F oven for 40 to 45 minutes, or until a toothpick inserted in the centre comes out clean. Allow cake to cool in pan.

To make sauce: In a small saucepan, melt the butter. Gradually stir in flour and sugars. Stir in cream. Cook over medium heat, stirring constantly, until smooth and thick. Stir in rum flavouring.

When cake is cool, turn out and serve with hot sauce on the side.

Makes one 9-inch cake.

Snitz and Knepp

A traditional Mennonite casserole, flavourful and hearty.

Snitz

2 cups dried apples	**2 tbsp. brown sugar**
1½ lbs. cured ham	

Knepp

2 cups all-purpose flour	**1 egg, beaten**
3½ tsp. baking powder	**2 tbsp. butter, melted**
½ tsp. salt	**⅓ to ½ cup milk**

To make snitz: Wash dried apples, place in a bowl, cover with water, and soak overnight.

Next day, in a large kettle, cover ham with cold water. Bring water to a boil; then cook slowly over low heat for 3 hours. Add apples and the water in which they soaked. Add brown sugar and cook for 1 more hour.

To make knepp: Sift together flour, baking powder, and salt. Stir in egg and melted butter. Add enough milk to make a batter stiff enough to drop from a spoon. Drop batter by spoonfuls into boiling ham and apples. Cover pan tightly and cook dumplings for 10 minutes without lifting the cover. If dumplings are not done, cover and cook for 2 more minutes. Serve immediately.

Serves 8.

Pork and Sauerkraut Goulash

This was the hit of the buffet table at a summer-in-the-country dinner party.

2 cups sauerkraut	1 can water
2½ cups chopped onion	1 tbsp. caraway seed
¼ cup vegetable oil	2 canned plum
2 cloves garlic,	tomatoes,
minced	seeded and
2 tbsp. sweet paprika	chopped
1 tsp. salt	¾ cup sour cream
3 lbs. boneless pork	¼ cup whipping (35%)
shoulder, cut into	cream
1-inch cubes	3 tbsp. minced parsley
1 10-oz. can beef	
consommé	

In a large bowl, cover sauerkraut with cold water and soak for 20 minutes, then drain and press out liquid. Set sauerkraut aside.

In a large ovenproof casserole, sauté the onion in the vegetable oil. Remove casserole from heat and add garlic, paprika, salt, and pork cubes. Pour in consommé and water; add caraway seeds and tomatoes. Bring to a boil over moderate heat, stirring occasionally. When liquid boils, stir in the sauerkraut and remove from heat.

Place casserole in preheated 325°F oven. Bake for 1 hour and 30 minutes, stirring occasionally.

Remove casserole from oven and place on burner over medium heat. Bring to a slow boil. Boil until most of the liquid has evaporated. (This will take 5 to 10 minutes.) Skim top occasionally to remove grease.

In a small bowl, whisk together the sour cream and cream. Stir the creams into the goulash. Cook over moderate heat, being careful not to let the cream boil, until slightly thickened, about 10 minutes. Sprinkle with chopped parsley. Serve immediately.

Serves 6.

Note: The casserole can be prepared in advance and refrigerated. After you have boiled out the excess liquid, remove casserole from heat and allow to cool. Refrigerate overnight. Before serving, reheat casserole, add cream and sour cream, and cook as directed.

Crackling Bread

"Put on de skillet, put on de lid, Mama's gonna make a little shortenin' bread." Try this on a wintry morning.

1 *lb. salt pork, pork fat, or beef suet*	1 *tsp. salt*
	½ *cup skim milk*
2 *cups cornmeal*	½ *cup cold water*
3 *tsp. baking powder*	1 *egg*

Cut the pork or beef suet into very small cubes. Heat a heavy 9-inch ovenproof skillet. Add pork or beef cubes, cover, and fry, stirring occasionally, until the fat has cooked out of the pork and the cubes are brown and very crisp. Lift out the "cracklings" with a slotted spoon and drain on paper towels. They should be about as big as peas. (If they're larger, cut them.) Drain fat from skillet and set the skillet aside.

In a mixing bowl, combine cornmeal, baking powder, and salt. Stir in the skim milk, water, and egg and beat until smooth. Stir in cracklings and pour the batter into the skillet. Bake in a preheated 400°F oven for 30 to 35 minutes, or until bread is golden brown. Serve hot.

Serves 8.

Choucroute Garnie

A gift to epicures from Alsace Lorraine.

2 large onions, peeled
  and quartered
2 tbsp. vegetable oil
6 medium-thick
  smoked loin
  pork chops
5 cups sauerkraut,
  drained
3 cooking apples,
  peeled, cored,
  and chopped
1 tsp. mustard

¼ cup brown sugar
4 large cloves garlic,
  peeled and
  crushed
¼ tsp. freshly ground
  black pepper
2½ cups dry white wine
2 lbs. sausages,
  kielbasa,
  knockwurst, or
  bratwurst
1 tbsp. vegetable oil

In a 6-quart ovenproof casserole on top of the stove over medium heat, cook the onions in the vegetable oil till onions are soft but not brown. Remove from heat. Set pork chops on top of onions.

In a large bowl, mix the sauerkraut, apples, mustard, brown sugar, garlic, and pepper. Pour sauerkraut mixture over pork chops; pour in the wine. Bake in a 350°F oven for about 3 hours. While pork chops are baking, prepare sausages. In a steamer rack over boiling water, steam sausages for 12 minutes. Fifteen minutes before chops are done, in a skillet, heat oil; add steamed sausages and brown, turning. To serve, place sauerkraut on a platter and arrange chops and sausages on top.

Serves 6.

Chicken Pistachio-Nut Roll-ups

The Niagara Peninsula is well known as the fruit belt, but to 17 per cent of Ontario's 132,000,000 kilos of poultry production, this verdant area is just chicken feed. These green-and-white pinwheels will be the hit of your summer entertaining.

2 whole chicken
    breasts, boned
    and cut in half
2 tbsp. chopped
    celery leaves
2 tbsp. chopped green
    onion or chives
2 tbsp. chopped parsley
4 tbsp. butter
1 cup pistachios, shelled
    and chopped

Salt
Pepper
2 slices white bread,
    torn into pieces
Milk
3 cloves garlic, crushed
    with skin on
Fresh celery leaves
Parsley

Place each chicken half-breast between two pieces of plastic wrap and pound flat with a bottle or mallet.

In a frying pan, sauté chopped celery leaves, green onion, and parsley in 2 tablespoons of the butter. Add chopped nuts, salt, and pepper. Add bread pieces and enough milk to make a smooth paste. Spread about 1 tablespoon of the warm paste on each chicken breast. (The paste should be spread as if you were buttering a piece of bread, or make a line of paste down the length of each piece of chicken and then spread thinly.) Starting with the end of the breast that has a bit of fat on it, roll each breast tightly and place seam-side down in a baking pan. Add garlic. Melt remaining 2 tablespoons of butter and pour over top. Bake, uncovered, in a 375°F oven for 20 minutes, then set pan in the refrigerator and allow to cool for at least 2 hours, or until completely chilled.

Using a very sharp knife, slice the rolled-up chicken breasts into half-inch rounds. Garnish with celery leaves and parsley.

Serves 4 as a main course or 8 as an appetizer.

Chicken Prince of Wales

The pretty nineteenth-century town of Niagara-on-the-Lake sits on the shores of Lake Ontario at the mouth of the Niagara River. From 1792 to 1796, it was the capital of Upper Canada. Fudge is still made on marble slabs, luscious jam is created from local fruit, and the Prince of Wales Hotel was host to royalty as far back as 1901.

4 whole chicken
   breasts, boned
   and cut in half
Salt
Pepper
1 cup all-purpose
   flour

4 eggs, beaten
¼ cup butter
2 tbsp. vegetable oil
1 cup pecans or
   hazelnuts,
   coarsely chopped

Sauce

2 tbsp. butter
2 tbsp. finely chopped
   shallots (or 2 tsp.
   finely chopped
   onion and 1 tsp.
   finely chopped
   garlic)

1 tbsp. Dijon mustard
¼ cup medium-dry
   white wine
2 cups whipping (35%)
   cream
Salt
Pepper

Season chicken breasts with salt and pepper, dredge lightly in flour, then dip into beaten eggs.

In a frying pan, heat butter and vegetable oil over medium heat. Sprinkle half the chopped nuts into the frying pan; then immediately set chicken breasts on nuts and press them down with a spatula. Sprinkle remaining nuts on top of chicken breasts. Turn breasts over to sear the other side.

In a jelly-roll pan, place chicken pieces in a single layer. Bake in a preheated 400°F oven for 10 to 15 minutes, depending on thickness of breasts, or until chicken is tender.

To make sauce: In a saucepan over medium heat, melt butter. Add chopped shallots and sauté for 3 minutes, being careful not to let the shallots brown. Stir in Dijon mustard; then add white wine and deglaze pan. Add cream and a pinch of salt and pepper. Reduce sauce by two-thirds. Correct seasoning to taste.

Place chicken pieces on a large platter. Pour sauce over chicken and serve immediately.

Serves 4.

Lemon Chicken Baked in a Bag

Before self-cleaning ovens and plastic grocery bags, roasting a chicken meant a grease-splattered oven and a crusted pan. Smart homemakers used simple ingenuity to create this tender, perfectly browned chicken – and saved themselves a lot of work.

1 lemon	1 tsp. salt
3 lb. fryer chicken	Paprika
1½ tsp. margarine	

Cut lemon in half and rub cut sides over the chicken. Rub margarine over the chicken. Salt the chicken inside and out and place half the lemon in the chicken cavity. Sprinkle the cavity and breast with paprika. Cross the chicken legs and tie them together; then tuck the wings behind the back.

Line the bottom of a large paper bag with one piece of waxed paper. (Do not allow the waxed paper to curl up the sides of the bag.) Place the bag on a rack in a shallow roasting pan.

Place the chicken on the waxed paper breast-side up. Spread the sides and top of the bag so the paper is not touching the chicken. Tie the bag shut with string, or fold the top and close it with staples or paper clips. Bake the chicken in a 425°F oven for 1 hour. Reduce the heat to 400°F and bake for 30 more minutes.

Remove roasting pan from oven and cut open the paper bag. Remove chicken, being careful not to spill the drippings. Cut chicken into quarters and serve with drippings.

Serves 4.

Party Pineapple-Chicken Curry

Prepare this dish fit for a Raj the night before and enjoy your own party – with no fuss in the kitchen.

2 medium onions,
  chopped
1 stalk celery, chopped
2 apples, unpeeled,
  cored, and
  thinly sliced
6 tbsp. butter
¼ cup all-purpose
  flour
4 tsp. curry powder
1½ tsp. salt
½ tsp. freshly ground
  black pepper

½ tsp. dry mustard
1 bay leaf
3 cups chicken broth
2 cups canned
  pineapple
  chunks
1 cup cereal (10%)
  cream
4 cups cooked chicken
  (1 whole chicken),
  cut into bite-sized
  chunks
3 tsp. Maggi liquid
  seasoning

In a very large skillet, sauté onion, celery, and apple slices in butter until tender (but not browned). Transfer to large saucepan. Sprinkle with flour and curry powder and cook for 3 minutes. Add salt, pepper, mustard, and bay leaf. Gradually stir in chicken broth and bring liquid to a boil. Simmer slowly for 15 minutes, stirring occasionally. Remove bay leaf. Add pineapple and cream and cook for 2 minutes. Cover and refrigerate.

Just before serving: Add chicken to refrigerated curry mixture. Cook until heated through, then stir in Maggi.

Serve over rice with chutney.

Serves 6.

Eggs Poached in Beaujolais Nouveau

Which came first? The chicken or the egg?

¼ cup softened butter
2 tbsp. all-purpose
   flour
12 baby onions, peeled,
   or 1 cup chopped
   onion
1 bottle Beaujolais
   Nouveau
1 clove garlic, crushed

Bouquet garni, made
   with 1 sprig
   thyme, ¼ bay leaf,
   1 stalk celery,
   and white part
   of 1 leek
Salt
Pepper
8 eggs

Place 2 tbsp. of the butter in a small bowl. Add flour and mix with fingers until smooth. Break the mixture into pea-sized pieces.

In a large frying pan, melt remaining 2 tbsp. butter. (Do not use an aluminum pan, as the aluminum may discolour the eggs.) Sauté the onions in the butter until they are golden. Then add the wine, garlic, bouquet garni, salt, and pepper. Turn heat to medium-high. As soon as the liquid starts to boil, lower the heat and simmer, uncovered, for 20 minutes. Lift the onions out with a slotted spoon and set aside. Liquid should still be simmering.

Break an egg into a cup, then slide it gently into the simmering liquid. If your pan is large enough, you can poach up to 4 eggs at a time. Poach eggs for 4 minutes, then lift them out of the pan with a slotted spoon. Place them on a plate and keep them warm while the second batch of eggs is poaching.

Once all the eggs are cooked, add the pea-sized flour-and-butter balls to the simmering liquid and bring liquid to a boil, stirring constantly, until liquid is thickened. Lower the heat and return sautéed onions to the pan to warm them. Add salt and pepper to taste.

Place 2 eggs on each plate; spoon sauce and onions around eggs.

Serves 4.

⚜ Mushroom Consommé

There are thirty-eight thousand kinds of mushrooms in the world. Scholars say that a certain hallucinogenic mushroom was the legendary "ambrosia" of the Greek gods; some modern-day enthusiasts in Mexico consume a strain of mushroom to reach "enlightenment." And what variety of mushroom did Alice in Wonderland munch on?

In Canada, the crop has mushroomed: we harvest eighty-six million pounds a year. To use up some of them, mushroom consommé makes a pungent, light first course, good with any meal.

1 2-oz. package dried Polish mushrooms	2 tsp. soy sauce
	3 egg whites
	2 egg shells, crumbled
6 cups chicken stock	3 cups water
1 lb. fresh mushrooms	Several drops of lemon juice
3 tbsp. minced shallot	
1 tsp. salt	Sliced mushroom caps or sliced lemon (garnish)
¼ tsp. pepper	
2 tbsp. dry sherry	

Wash mushrooms well, twice. In a large saucepan, soak dried mushrooms in chicken stock for about 2 hours, or until mushrooms are soft. Separate caps and stems of fresh mushrooms. Slice the caps and mince the stems. Set sliced caps aside. Remove dried mushrooms from stock with a slotted spoon. Discard any hard pieces, then mince mushrooms. Return to saucepan. Add fresh minced mushroom stems, shallot, salt, and pepper. Bring to a boil over medium-high heat; reduce heat and let simmer for about 40 minutes, skimming occasionally. Keep level of liquid constant by adding water. Remove from heat and stir in sherry and soy sauce.

In a 4-quart stainless-steel bowl, beat egg whites with eggshells until whites are frothy. Whisking constantly, gradually add hot broth to whites. When mixed, return to saucepan, place over medium heat, and whisk gently until liquid is simmering. Let simmer, without stirring, for 15 minutes. Do not allow liquid to boil. Egg whites will coagulate and float to the top, forming a cap.

While liquid is simmering, line a strainer or sieve with two layers of cheesecloth. Set strainer over a large bowl. Gently ladle consommé mixture into strainer. Press liquid through cheesecloth with the back of the ladle. Taste broth and adjust seasoning.

In a small saucepan, combine water and lemon juice. Bring to a boil. Add sliced mushroom caps and boil for 2 minutes. Drain mushrooms well, then place them in a clean saucepan and add strained consommé. Heat just until consommé begins to simmer. Ladle into bowls and garnish with mushroom caps or paper-thin slices of lemon.

Serves 8.

Scotch Eggs

Tuck these into the family's lunch bags or into your picnic basket.

6 hard-cooked eggs	1 tbsp. chervil
1 lb. pork-sausage meat	2 tbsp. tarragon
	½ tsp. salt
1 tbsp. breadcrumbs	Freshly ground pepper
3 tbsp. finely chopped parsley	¼ cup all-purpose flour
1 medium onion, peeled and minced	1 cup vegetable oil

Remove shells from eggs. In a bowl, mix sausage, breadcrumbs, parsley, onion, chervil, tarragon, salt, and pepper. Coat each egg completely with sausage mixture. (Coating should be about one-half inch thick, and even all around.) Roll egg lightly in flour. In a large skillet, heat oil. Fry coated eggs, turning to brown evenly on all sides, for about 10 minutes. Cool. Slice in half and serve. To store, wrap individually in plastic wrap.

Serves 6.

Apple-Cheese Coffee Cake

It's a treat to stop at a roadside fruit stand and buy a basket of apples fresh-picked from a farmer's orchard. Great eating. In 1810 an American, John McIntosh, followed the apple of his eye to Upper Canada. Sadly, the lady died before he arrived. But he decided to stay and set about clearing land in Dundas County. He found twenty small trees bearing sweet red apples, which became known as McIntosh. McIntosh apples are still being grown by his descendants, and are eaten all over the world.

Crust

1 ¼ cups all-purpose
  flour
1 ¼ tsp. baking
  powder
⅓ cup sugar

⅛ tsp. salt
⅓ cup cold butter
1 egg
1 tbsp. milk
½ tsp. vanilla

Filling

1 cup ricotta cheese
1 8-oz. package cream
  cheese
4 eggs
¾ cup sugar
1 cup whipping (35%)
  cream

2 tsp. vanilla
3 apples
3 tbsp. butter
⅔ cup sugar
1 tsp. vanilla
Whole pecans

To make crust: In a food processor, place flour, baking powder, sugar, and salt. Cut cold butter into small pieces and add to food processor. Using quick on-and-off bursts, process until dough is crumbly.

In a small bowl, beat together egg, milk, and vanilla. With food processor on, pour egg mixture through funnel. Continue to process just until dough leaves sides of bowl. Remove dough from food processor and form into a ball. Wrap in plastic wrap and chill for 30 minutes. When chilled, roll out dough and press on sides and bottom of a 10-inch spring-form pan.

To make filling: In the food processor, process cheeses, eggs, and sugar. Add cream and vanilla. Pour mixture into dough-lined pan. Bake in a 350°F oven for 1 hour and 15 minutes, or until cake is set. Turn off heat. Cool cake in the oven for 30 minutes.

While cake is cooling, peel and core apples and cut into ½-inch-thick slices. In a large saucepan, melt butter. Stir in sugar and vanilla. Add apple slices and cook until apple slices are glazed. Arrange apples and glaze on cheesecake in overlapping rows. Top with nuts. Chill. Serve cold.

Makes 1 cake.

Sour-Cream Spice Cake

A fast-and-easy coffee cake with a spicy aroma.

1 cup brown sugar, firmly packed	½ tsp. cream of tartar
1 large egg	1 tsp. baking soda
1 cup sour cream	1 tsp. cinnamon
1½ cups sifted all-purpose flour	½ tsp. nutmeg
½ cup raisins	¼ tsp. cloves
	½ tsp. salt

In a large mixing bowl, beat together sugar and egg. Mix in sour cream. Stir in flour, then add raisins, cream of tartar, baking soda, cinnamon, nutmeg, cloves, and salt, and mix well. Spread batter evenly in a greased 9-inch-square pan.

Bake in a preheated 350°F oven for 35 minutes, or until toothpick inserted in centre of cake comes out clean. Remove from oven and let cool.

This cake is good sprinkled with icing sugar.

Makes one 9-inch cake.

Dundee Cake

This rich fruit cake is always proper for an auspicious occasion. Tradition requires the almond pattern, baked on the top.

½ cup white raisins
½ cup dark raisins
½ cup currants
¼ cup candied fruit
  peel
6 candied cherries,
  finely chopped
½ cup ground almonds
1 cup butter
1 cup sugar

Grated rind of
  1 orange
4 eggs, beaten
2¼ cups all-purpose
  flour
1 tsp. baking powder
1 tbsp. sherry
¼ cup blanched
  almonds

In a small bowl, combine raisins, currants, candied peel, cherries, and ground almonds.

In a large mixing bowl, cream the butter and sugar; stir in orange rind. Gradually add eggs and beat well. Combine flour and baking powder and fold into the butter-egg mixture. Add sherry; stir in dried fruit.

Grease a 10-inch angel-food pan and line with waxed paper. Pour batter into cake pan. Arrange blanched almonds in circles on top of batter. Bake in a 300°F oven for 2 to 2½ hours, or until a knife inserted in the centre of the cake comes out clean.

Allow cake to cool in the pan for 10 minutes, then turn onto a wire rack. Cool completely before slicing.

Makes one 10-inch cake.

Sir Walter Scott's Cock-a-Leekie

Immigrants from Scotland settled in Cambridge and Fergus, and every summer these two towns host Highland games. After watching the caber toss, sword dancing, and pipe-and-drum competitions, you'll be ready to enjoy some dishes with a decidedly Scottish brogue like cock-a-leekie, Sir Walter Scott's favourite potage.

1 3-lb. stewing chicken	1 tbsp. salt
6 leeks, washed, trimmed, and cut into 1-inch slices	1 lb. pitted prunes
	Salt
	Pepper
½ cup rice	½ cup chopped parsley
2 parsnips, peeled and trimmed	

Place chicken in a large soup pot. Cover with water and bring to a boil. Add leeks, rice, parsnips, and salt. Cover the pot and simmer gently for 2 hours. Add the prunes and continue to simmer for another 30 minutes.

Remove pot from the heat and lift out chicken. When it is cool enough to handle, remove the skin and cut the meat into thin slices. Return the meat slices to the soup. Season broth to taste with salt and pepper. To serve, sprinkle with parsley.

Serves 8.

Creamed Finnan Haddie

Try this tasty casserole at your next Sunday brunch.

2 lbs. smoked haddock
Water and milk, to
cover
3 tbsp. butter
3 tbsp. all-purpose
flour

½ cup whipping (35%)
cream
Freshly ground black
pepper
Nutmeg
Buttered toast

Soak haddock in water for 2 hours. Drain haddock and place in a saucepan; cover with equal amounts of water and milk. Bring liquid to a boil. Remove from heat and let stand for 15 minutes. Drain haddock, reserving stock.

In the top of a double boiler, melt the butter. Stir in flour and cook over hot water for 3 minutes, stirring continuously. Add cream and 2 cups of the reserved haddock stock. Continue to cook, stirring from time to time, for about 5 minutes, or until sauce is thick. Season to taste with pepper and nutmeg.

Remove skin and bones from haddock. Break the meat of the haddock into pieces. Fold pieces into sauce and simmer gently for 4 to 5 minutes, or until fish is heated through.

Serve in a shallow casserole surrounded by triangles of buttered toast.

Serves 6.

Gaspé Biscuits

A century ago there was a mixture of English, Irish, and Scottish people in the Gaspé Peninsula. Aunt Alma made bread with her own potato-and-hop yeast; she also made these Gaspé biscuits, which were a popular tea-time dainty. Happily, the recipe made its way to St. Catharines.

4 cups all-purpose
   flour
1½ tsp. salt
4 tsp. baking powder
1 cup raisins
1 cup margarine or
   shortening

1½ cups sugar
2 eggs, beaten
1½ tsp. vanilla
1 tsp. baking soda
1 cup buttermilk

In a bowl, combine flour, salt, and baking powder. Stir in raisins.

In a large mixing bowl, cream together margarine and sugar. Beat in eggs and vanilla. Dissolve baking soda in buttermilk and beat in.

Add flour and raisins to buttermilk batter. Make a dough stiff enough to roll. (You may need to add more flour.) On a lightly floured surface, roll out dough until it is one-half inch thick.

With a sharp knife, cut rolled dough into 3-inch squares. Place squares of dough on an ungreased cookie sheet and bake in a 375°F oven for 30 to 40 minutes, or until biscuits are golden brown.

Makes about 4 dozen biscuits.

Note: Biscuits are also good with currants or fresh blueberries. Replace the raisins with 2 cups currants or blueberries.

Poached Salmon with Raspberries

A dramatic way to raise the flavour of fresh-poached fish to great heights.

2 tbsp. chopped shallots	½ cup fresh raspberries
2 tbsp. unsalted butter	1½ cups whipping (35%) cream
¾ cup white wine	Salt
½ cup water	Pepper
6 6-oz. salmon fillets	Mint leaf

In a large frying pan, sauté the shallots in the butter until shallots are tender. Add wine and water and turn heat to high. As soon as liquids begin to boil, reduce heat to low so that liquids simmer.

Place the salmon fillets side by side in the simmering liquid and cook on very low heat for 7 to 12 minutes, depending on the thickness of the fillets. Be careful not to overcook. Remove the salmon from the liquid and cover with foil to keep warm.

Add most of the raspberries (save a few for garnish) and the cream to the saucepan. Turn heat to high and boil the sauce until it thickens and is creamy, about 3 minutes. Season with salt and pepper, then strain through a sieve onto a serving plate. Arrange the salmon on top of the sauce and decorate with the remaining whole raspberries and a mint leaf.

Serves 6.

Port Dover French-Fried Perch

There's a reason Port Dover boasts one of the world's largest fresh-water fishing fleets. And that reason is perch. You can eat a mess of crispy, pan-fried perch every day for a week in Port Dover, and never find the same recipe twice.

2 *cups all-purpose*	*Salt*
flour	*Pepper*
2 *tsp. baking powder*	1 *bottle beer*
1 *tsp. baking soda*	2 *eggs*
2 *tbsp. cornmeal*	4 *lbs. perch fillets*

In a large bowl, combine flour, baking powder, soda, cornmeal, salt, and pepper. Slowly stir in beer and eggs until you have a thick batter.

Dip fish in batter. In a deep-fryer or in a pot with at least 4 inches of vegetable oil, deep-fry fish for approximately 8 minutes, or until golden brown.

Serve with French fries.

Serves 8.

Pickled Pumpkin

Enjoy the fruits of autumn all year round with this tasty orange pickle. This is a perfect condiment for fried fish.

1 5 *to* 6 *lb. pumpkin*	1 *tbsp. crumbled*
2 *cups cider vinegar*	*cinnamon stick*
3 *lbs. sugar*	2 *pieces crystallized*
1 *tsp. whole cloves*	*ginger*

Remove skin and seeds from pumpkin and cut into 1-inch cubes.

In a large saucepan, bring the vinegar and sugar to a boil and simmer until the sugar is dissolved. Place the cloves, cinnamon, and ginger in a cheesecloth bag. Add to the vinegar-sugar syrup and boil for 5 minutes. Add the pumpkin cubes and bring the mixture to a fast, rolling boil. Boil for 25 minutes, stirring often. Remove the spice bag.

Ladle pumpkin into sterilized jars and pour the vinegar syrup on top to completely cover pumpkin. Seal jars.

Makes 10 to 12 cups.

CHAPTER 3

LAKES AND BAYS

*Carved out of the Pre-Cambrian
Shield, the road meanders through the
Georgian Lakelands. In summer, it's cottage
country, with camp grounds, nature trails, canoeing and
fishing, and the call of the loon across the lake. Then,
when winter blankets the landscape with snow, the ski
slopes and snowmobile trails beckon. It's year-round
vacation country – only the menu changes.*

Recipes

Restaurants of the Region

ALLISTON

Nottawasaga Inn • A large family resort with everything from tennis and racquet-ball courts, horseback riding, cross-country skiing, swimming, an eighteen-hole golf course, and one of the finest and prettiest dining rooms in the area

BARRIE

Brittons • An elegant blue-and-white-painted brick mansion circled with an inviting verandah. Built around 1906, the house is still embellished by the original stained glass window, wooden panelling, and staircases.

La Fayette • Another gourmet restaurant with several posh rooms

COLLINGWOOD

Spike & Spoon • A popular spot with standard well-done continental fare. Light, delicious meals and yummy desserts

FRYING PAN ISLAND

Henry's • For fish that goes from the water to the frying pan, go to Henry's, a boat trip from Midland

GRAVENHURST

Ascona Place • This dining room could be considered tops anywhere in the world. Large menu, patio, and formal dining with a summer beer garden. Exceptional wine list. One of the three best restaurants in rural Ontario

HUNTSVILLE

Deerhurst Inn • A huge family resort complex with full facilities, entertainment, and dining

MEAFORD

Backstreet Café • Excellent food and casual family fare in an easygoing atmosphere

MIDLAND

Frieda's • An old house with a classic menu

ORILLIA

Ossawippi Express • Four "railway cars" presided over by an ex-Ascona Place chef. Ambitious menu with excellent renditions

Paul Webber's Drive In • Under a bridge over the highway, travellers from both directions can enjoy made-to-order burgers, fries, and shakes

OWEN SOUND

Clarenville • Fresh fish

The Clog & Thistle • Lots of flaming dishes and a continental menu

Norma Jean's • Chicken wings, sandwiches, and salads

PORT CARLING

Sherwood Inn • Water-skiing and boating in summer and snowmobiling in winter. A lovely large dining room that's at its best with fresh produce

PORT SEVERN

Arrowood Lodge • German homecooking plus accommodation

STAYNER

Old Dutch Inn • Indonesian cooking

Green Tomato Mincemeat

Group of Seven painters A.Y. Jackson, Arthur Lismer, and Tom Thomson etched many of Muskoka's scenes into our consciousness, but they never told us that there's honey in the heart of "cottage country." Grandmother's favourite medicine is a spoonful of honey. Around Midland, Orillia, and Lindsay, the bees have been busy as – well, bees. Every queen bee lays about two thousand eggs a day, and five hundred worker bees give up their lives to produce each pound of liquid gold.

3 *quarts green tomatoes*	**1** *tsp. salt*
8 *cups cold water*	**1** *tsp. cinnamon*
1 *cup margarine*	**1** *tsp. nutmeg*
4 *cups raisins*	**1** *tsp. mace*
2 *cups currants*	**1** *tsp. cloves*
½ *cup vinegar*	**3¾** *cups honey*

Wash and dry green tomatoes. In a meat grinder with a coarse blade, grind tomatoes, or chop them coarsely in a food processor. In a large kettle, bring water to a boil. Add ground tomatoes and boil for 1 hour. Pour into a fine-mesh plastic colander and allow to drain overnight.

In a large enamel kettle, combine drained tomato pulp, margarine, raisins, currants, vinegar, salt, cinnamon, nutmeg, mace, and cloves. Bring to a boil, reduce heat, cover, and simmer for 2 hours.

Add honey and cook for 15 minutes more, stirring frequently. Pour into sterilized jars and seal.

Makes 8 cups.

Mincemeat Chiffon Pie

Honey has a sweetness that mellows the green tomatoes to make a delicious pie.

1 envelope gelatin	3 egg whites
⅓ cup water	2 tbsp. honey
¼ cup rum or apple juice	Pinch salt
1½ cups Green Tomato Mince-meat (see p. 83)	1 cup whipping (35%) cream
	1 baked 10-inch pie shell (see p. 95)

In a saucepan, sprinkle gelatin in water and allow gelatin to soften. Place over low heat and cook until gelatin is dissolved.

In a large mixing bowl, combine rum and Green Tomato Mincemeat. Add gelatin. Place bowl in refrigerator and chill for about 25 minutes, or until mixture forms mounds when dropped from a spoon.

In a separate bowl, beat egg whites until stiff. Slowly beat in honey and salt. Fold into chilled mincemeat mixture. Whip cream and fold into mincemeat. Pour mincemeat into baked pie shell. Chill until firm, about 3 hours.

Makes one 10-inch pie.

Orange Honey Cake

Since ancient times, honey has been prized as an aid to health and beauty. After fifty centuries, we still don't know why it's so darn good for us. Used in baking, it keeps a cake moist.

¼ cup light vege-
    table oil
¾ cup liquid or solid
    honey
¾ cup sugar
2 eggs
½ cup orange
    marmalade
2 cups sifted all-
    purpose flour

2 tsp. baking
    powder
1 tsp. baking soda
½ tsp. salt
¼ tsp. freshly grated
    nutmeg
¼ tsp. mace
½ tsp. cinnamon
1 cup very strong
    orange-spice
    tea, cooled

In the large bowl of an electric mixer, combine oil, honey, sugar, eggs, and marmalade, and beat on high speed for 2 minutes.

In a separate bowl, mix together flour, baking powder, soda, salt, nutmeg, mace, and cinnamon. Turn mixer to low speed and add dry ingredients alternately with cold tea. Mix just until dry ingredients are blended in; do not overbeat.

Pour batter into a greased 9-inch-square pan and bake in a 325°F oven, on the middle rack, for 1 hour and 10 minutes.

Makes one 9-inch cake.

Potato Gratin

City folk and trend-setters have relegated the potato to the basement of chic. Potatoes cause panic to dieters. The familiar "scoop of mashed" has disappeared from most restaurant menus. But to the folks in Alliston, the fifty-million-dollar crop of this gentle tuber is no small potatoes. In one of its versatile forms or another, we all still love spuds. Potato gratin is an oldie but a goodie.

5 medium potatoes	**¾ cup whipping (35%)**
2 cloves garlic,	**cream**
finely chopped	**¼ lb. Gruyère**
1 cup milk	**cheese, grated**
Salt, pepper, and	**¼ cup butter**
nutmeg to	
taste	

Peel potatoes and cut them in thin slices. (Do not wash them: washing removes the starch.) Place in a large, heatproof casserole. Add garlic, milk, salt, pepper, and nutmeg. Mix well. Bring to a boil on high heat. Boil until the starch of the potatoes has slightly thickened the milk. Stir in half the cream and again bring to a boil, then remove from the heat.

In a baking dish, arrange the potatoes in layers. Pour in the rest of the cream and gently work it under the potatoes. Bake, uncovered, in a 325°F oven for about 1½ hours, or until golden brown.

Preheat the broiler. Sprinkle the potatoes with grated Gruyère, dot with butter, and place under the broiler for about 2 minutes, or until golden brown. Serve immediately.

Serves 6.

Warm Potato-and-Leek Salad

We are a nation of potato eaters. Nothing says "home cooking" more honestly than a platter of baked, boiled, steamed, or mashed potatoes. Summer would be incomplete without potato salad.

4 leeks	**1 tbsp. tarragon**
2 tbsp. corn oil	**vinegar**
12 new red potatoes,	**⅓ cup packed fresh**
scrubbed but	**parsley**
not peeled	**Salt**
Sprig of mint	**Freshly ground**
⅔ cup sour cream	**black pepper**

Remove any dark-green parts from leeks. Cut leeks through the centre and rinse well under cold running water to remove all sand. Chop into half-inch pieces. In a large heavy skillet, heat the oil; add the leeks and cook over medium-high heat for 2 minutes. Lower heat, cover, and cook for about 10 minutes more, or until leeks are soft.

While leeks are cooking, place potatoes and mint in a large pot of boiling water. Cook, covered, over medium heat until potatoes are fork-tender. Turn off the heat; drain potatoes well and return them to the pan. Place pan on cooling stove element to evaporate all moisture.

Add leeks to potatoes and stir gently. Fold in the sour cream and vinegar. Heat, but be careful not to let the cream boil. Add chopped parsley, then salt and pepper to taste.

Serve warm. This salad is good with fresh sliced tomatoes.

Serves 6.

Steamed Whitefish with Egg Sauce

In summer, the Muskokas, Georgian Bay, and Barrie resound with the laughter of children and the call of the loon. Lakes and bays are awash with sailboats and speedboats.

The pleasures of cooking don't melt away with the snow – they just move outdoors. Aromatic smoke from barbecues and camp-fires drifts across the lakes, and weekend fishermen know there's an easy catch of whitefish and walleye.

**1 2- to 3-lb. whole
  whitefish
1 clove garlic, minced
Salt
Freshly ground black
  pepper
3 tbsp. butter
3 tbsp. flour**

**1 ½ cups milk
3 hard-cooked eggs,
  coarsely chopped
½ tsp. Worcestershire
  sauce
2 tbsp. lemon juice
1 tsp. Dijon mustard
Chopped parsley**

Place the fish on a large piece of cheesecloth. Sprinkle with garlic, salt, and pepper. Cover fish with another piece of cheesecloth, and wrap cheesecloth around fish. In a deep roasting pan, place wrapped fish on a rack and add about one-half inch of water to the pan. Bring to a boil, reduce heat, cover, and steam for 15 minutes. Remove cheesecloth and set fish on a hot platter. Keep warm.

In a saucepan, melt the butter. Add flour and stir with a wire whisk until blended.

In a separate saucepan, heat the milk. Add hot milk all at once to the butter-flour mixture and stir vigorously with the whisk until the sauce is thickened and smooth. Add chopped eggs, Worcestershire sauce, lemon juice, mustard, salt, and pepper. Pour sauce over fish, sprinkle with parsley, and serve immediately.

Serves 4 to 6.

Mustard Relish

This relish is delicious with barbecued hamburgers and hot dogs.

4 cups shredded cabbage	2 cups all-purpose flour
4 cups diced green tomatoes	8 cups vinegar
4 cups diced cucumbers	2 tbsp. celery seed
4 cups diced onions	2 tbsp. turmeric
1 cup salt	1½ tbsp. dry mustard
	6 cups sugar

In a large container, place cabbage, tomatoes, cucumbers, and onions. Cover with salt. Add enough water to cover vegetables. Let stand for at least 12 hours.

Drain mixture. Place vegetables in a saucepan and cover with boiling water. Simmer for 10 minutes, then drain well.

In a large bowl, mix flour, 2 cups of the vinegar, celery seed, turmeric, and mustard until well combined. In a large saucepan, bring sugar and remaining 6 cups vinegar to a boil. Gradually stir in flour-vinegar mixture. When thoroughly mixed, add vegetables, bring to a boil again, reduce heat, and simmer for 10 minutes.

Cool slightly. Place vegetables in sterilized jars and cover with liquid, leaving a three-eighths-inch headspace. Seal.

Makes 12 to 15 jars.

Shepherd's Pie

Snow bunnies and athletes take to the hills in winter. They go cross-country and alpine skiing, snowmobiling and ice fishing. They load their cars with gear and hearty made-ahead casseroles.

4 large baking potatoes
3 tbsp. butter
1 tbsp. minced green-onion tops
¼ tsp. dried tarragon
Salt
Freshly ground pepper
1 egg yolk, beaten
2 tbsp. oil
1 large onion, chopped
8 mushrooms, cut into quarters

1½ lbs. lean leg of lamb, cut into small cubes
3 to 6 tbsp. beef stock
¼ tsp. Worcestershire sauce
2 tbsp. dry red wine
⅛ tsp. dried tarragon
Salt
Pepper
Butter

Scrub potatoes and bake in their skins in a 425°F oven for 45 to 60 minutes, or until tender. Remove from oven and allow to cool slightly. Cut potatoes in half and scoop pulp into a large bowl. Add butter, green onion, tarragon, salt, and pepper and blend well. Cool to lukewarm, then add egg yolk and beat in thoroughly. Set aside.

In a large skillet over medium-high heat, heat oil. Add onion and mushrooms and sauté until softened. Increase heat to high and add lamb cubes. Sauté for 2 minutes. Stir in beef stock, Worcestershire sauce, red wine, and tarragon. Remove from heat and add salt and pepper to taste.

Spread about two-thirds of the potato mixture over bottom and sides of a buttered 1½-quart baking dish with deep sides. Add sautéed lamb and all juices from skillet. Spread remaining potatoes evenly over top, covering lamb completely. Dot with butter and bake in a 375°F oven for about 1 hour and 30 minutes, or until top is golden brown and crispy.

Serves 6.

Note: Potato skins can be frozen. To serve, thaw, then cut into small pieces and deep-fry. They may be served as an appetizer.

This recipe can also be made with ground lamb. Add ¾ cup of the mashed potato to sautéed lamb before placing in baking dish.

Black Jack Bar-B-Q Short Ribs

This is the richest, tangiest barbecue sauce I have ever tasted. Ribs are a perfect dish to prepare in the city and take with you for a country weekend supper.

1 cup strong black coffee	**½ cup brown sugar**
1 cup Worcestershire sauce	**3 tbsp. chili powder**
	2 tsp. salt
1 cup ketchup	**2 cups chopped onion**
½ cup cider vinegar	**6 cloves garlic, minced**
	5 lbs. beef short ribs

In a large saucepan, combine coffee, Worcestershire sauce, ketchup, vinegar, sugar, chili powder, salt, onion, and garlic. Simmer for 25 minutes. Transfer mixture to a blender or food processor and purée. You will have about 5 cups of sauce.

Place ribs in a large flat pan. Pour 3 cups of the sauce over the ribs, turning ribs to coat with sauce. Pierce meat with a large fork. Marinate for 8 hours, turning once. Remove ribs from marinade and brush off excess liquid.

Bake ribs in a 350°F oven for 1 hour and 30 minutes. Heat remaining 2 cups of sauce and serve on the side. Marinade can be stored in the refrigerator.

Serves 6.

Butter Tarts

Besides the festival of humorous literature that has made Orillia famous, the town is held in high esteem for its most eloquently edible asset – butter tarts. In 1979, a national poll concluded that Wilkie's Bakery, on Colborne Street, makes the ultimate butter tart. A bronze plaque in the bakery attests to that.

½ cup raisins
¼ cup soft butter
¼ cup brown sugar
Pinch salt

½ cup corn syrup
1 egg, lightly beaten
½ tsp. vanilla
Pie Pastry (see p. 95)

In a small bowl, cover raisins with hot water and let stand for about 30 minutes.

In a large bowl, mix butter, brown sugar, salt, and corn syrup. Stir until sugar is dissolved and butter is creamed. Add egg and vanilla and mix well.

To make tart shells, line 16 medium-sized muffin cups with pie pastry. Distribute plumped raisins equally among tart shells, then fill with butter-sugar mixture. Bake in a 400°F oven for 15 to 20 minutes, or until the filling is lightly browned but still bubbling. Let tarts cool in pans for about 10 minutes, then remove from pans and cool on racks.

Makes 16 tarts.

Christmas Cake

Baking is a rewarding pastime during those long winter months in Muskoka.

1 lb. raisins	½ tsp. nutmeg
½ lb. currants	½ tsp. cloves
½ lb. glace cherries	¾ cup butter or
¼ lb. candied peel	margarine
½ lb. almonds or	1 cup brown sugar
pecans, halved	4 eggs
¼ cup dark rum	¼ cup molasses
2 cups all-purpose flour	¼ cup orange juice
1 tsp. salt	or rum
1 tsp. cinnamon	1 tbsp. orange rind

In a large bowl, mix together raisins, currants, glace cherries, peel, and nuts. Pour in rum and let soak overnight.

The next day, mix together flour, salt, cinnamon, nutmeg, and cloves. Stir flour mixture into soaked fruit.

In a mixing bowl, cream together butter and brown sugar. Add eggs one at a time, beating well after each addition. Stir in molasses, orange juice or rum, and orange rind, then pour into fruit-and-flour mixture and mix well.

Line two 8 by 4-inch loaf pans with white shelf paper. Grease the paper well. Pour batter into prepared pans and spread it smooth. Moisten top with a few drops of warm water and cover pans with aluminum foil. Line a cookie sheet with several layers of foil. Place cakes on top of foil-lined sheet and bake in a 350°F oven for 1 hour. Turn oven down to 300°F and bake for 2 more hours.

Remove cakes from oven and cool for 5 minutes, then remove cake from pans and cool on racks. When cool, wrap the cakes in rum-soaked cheesecloth and then in aluminum foil. Age for 4 to 6 weeks in refrigerator before using. This cake freezes well.

Makes 2 cakes.

Black Forest Cherry Kuchen

Once, Grossmutter baked this rich confection in Silesia (sometimes a part of Germany, sometimes Poland). Happily, this recipe has found a new home in a cheery kitchen in St. Thomas.

Cake

4 small eggs, separated
4 tbsp. warm water
⅔ cup sugar
1 tsp. vanilla
1½ tsp. almond extract
¼ tsp. cinnamon

Pinch salt
¾ cup all-purpose flour
⅓ cup cornstarch
3 tbsp. cocoa
2 tsp. baking powder
2 tsp. sugar

Filling

1 14-oz. can sour
    cherries
2 tbsp. sugar
Cold water
1½ tbsp. cornstarch
½ tsp. almond extract
1 cup whipping (35%)
    cream

1 tsp. sugar
½ tsp. vanilla
Semi-sweet chocolate
    shavings
Chocolate sprinkles

In a large mixing bowl, combine egg yolks and warm water and beat until foamy. Slowly add ⅔ cup sugar, vanilla, almond extract, cinnamon, and salt. Beat until white and fluffy.

In a separate bowl, mix flour, cornstarch, cocoa, and baking powder. In a small bowl, beat egg whites until foamy and gradually add 2 tsp. sugar. Continue to beat until stiff peaks form.

Fold egg whites into yolk-sugar mixture. Sift flour mixture over top and mix very lightly with a wooden spoon.

Grease the bottom of a 9-inch spring-form pan and dust with flour. Pour in batter. Bake in a 325°F oven for 30 minutes; then turn off the oven, leaving cake in for 5 minutes more.

Remove cake from oven and run a knife around the outside edge, then remove ring and let cake cool for several hours.

To serve: Drain cherries and pour juice into a saucepan. Add 2 tbsp. sugar to the juice and bring to a boil. In a small bowl, add enough cold water to the cornstarch to make a thick paste; stir paste into cherry juice. Boil until thick, then remove from heat and add cherries and almond extract.

Whip cream with 1 tsp. sugar and vanilla extract.

Cut cake in half. Cover cut half of cake with all the cherries and half the whipped cream. Replace top of cake and ice top and sides with remaining whipped cream. Sprinkle top of cake with chocolate shavings; cover sides with chocolate sprinkles.

Makes one 9-inch cake.

Pie Pastry

An easy, versatile, and tasty pastry.

2 cups all-purpose flour	**7 tbsp. Crisco**
½ tsp. salt	**3 tbsp. butter**
	¼ cup ice water

Sift together flour and salt. Using a pastry blender or two knives, cut in shortening and butter. Add the ice water a little at a time, blending well with a fork. Form dough into a ball. Dough can be rolled out and used immediately, or wrapped in waxed paper and refrigerated or frozen.

Makes pastry for a 2-crust pie.

Whole-Wheat Pumpkin Muffins

A quick-energy, satisfying breakfast or snack.

1½ cups whole-wheat flour	2 eggs
1½ tsp. baking powder	¾ cup cooked mashed pumpkin
½ tsp. baking soda	½ cup vegetable oil
½ tsp. salt	¾ cup brown sugar, well packed
½ tsp. cinnamon	¼ cup apple juice or orange juice
¼ tsp. nutmeg	
Pinch ground cloves	

In a large bowl, combine flour, baking powder, soda, salt, cinnamon, nutmeg, and cloves.

In a separate bowl, beat eggs lightly. Add pumpkin, oil, sugar, and juice and stir until well combined. Add egg-and-pumpkin mixture to flour mixture, stirring only until blended. Do not beat or overmix.

Spoon batter into greased muffin tins, filling each cup about two-thirds full. Bake in a 400°F oven for 20 minutes, or until toothpick inserted in centre of muffin comes out clean.

Makes 12 to 14 large muffins.

Note: You can substitute an equal amount of canned pumpkin for the fresh pumpkin.

Hot-and-Sour Soup

Doctor Norman Bethune, the great humanitarian, poet, soldier, lecturer, and theorist, won international fame as a thoracic surgeon and as the developer of the mobile blood bank in the Spanish Civil War. His selfless medical work in China made him a hero in that land, far from his home in Gravenhurst. Bethune's birthplace is a shrine for visitors from China.

To honour him, a Chinese recipe for a spicy broth.

4 *dried black Chinese mushrooms*	6 *cups chicken consommé*
⅛ *lb. lean pork*	¼ *cup bamboo shoots, cut into strips*
2 *tbsp. cornstarch*	8 *raw shrimp*
4 *tbsp. water*	1 *green onion, minced*
3 *tbsp. white vinegar*	6 *snow peas, whole or halved*
1 *tbsp. soy sauce*	1 *tsp. Tabasco*
¼ *tsp. salt*	2 *eggs, lightly beaten*
¼ *tsp. white pepper*	

In a small bowl, cover the mushrooms with boiling water. Let stand for 30 minutes. Drain the mushrooms and squeeze out excess liquid. Discard the stems; cut the caps into thin strips.

Cut the pork across the grain in quarter-inch-thick slices, then cut the slices into quarter-inch strips.

In a cup, combine the cornstarch and water and blend well. In another cup, combine the vinegar, soy sauce, salt, and pepper.

In a soup kettle, bring the chicken consommé to a boil. Add pork, bamboo shoots, and mushrooms. Bring to a boil again, then reduce heat to medium and add the shrimp.

Stir the vinegar-soy-sauce mixture and add to the soup. Stir the cornstarch mixture and stir it into the soup. Continue stirring until the soup thickens, about 2 minutes. Add the green onion, snow peas, and Tabasco.

Stirring constantly, pour beaten eggs into the soup in a thin stream. Serve at once.

Serves 4.

Duckling Breast with Elder Sauce For Two

Gourmet dining is at home in the country as well as the city. Several world-class chefs have made dining at country inns an epicurean's delight.

1 cup red wine
4 tsp. cognac
1 whole clove
1 bay leaf
1 tsp. chopped fresh basil or ½ tsp. dried basil
½ tsp. dried thyme

1 boneless duckling breast (about ½ lb.)
¼ cup elder berries
Salt
Freshly ground pepper
2 tbsp. butter
½ cup whipping (35%) cream

In a large bowl, combine red wine, 2 tsp. of the cognac, clove, bay leaf, basil, and thyme. Place duckling breast in the marinade and marinate in the refrigerator for 24 hours.

In a food processor, purée elder berries, or mash them well, and set aside. Take breast out of marinade and pat dry. Sprinkle with salt and pepper.

In a medium skillet, melt 1 tablespoon of the butter. Fry duckling breast for about 5 minutes on each side. Remove breast to a serving platter and keep warm.

Deglaze the skillet by pouring in the remaining 2 tsp. of cognac. Cook over medium-high heat, scraping up any browned bits from the skillet. Add the cream and cook over medium heat until sauce is reduced by half. Add elder-berry pureé to sauce and season with pepper.

Place a fine sieve over a saucepan and press sauce through the sieve with the back of a wooden spoon. Place saucepan over low heat and whip in remaining 1 tablespoon butter.

To serve, cut breast into 4 slices and ladle sauce over duck.

Serves 2.

Veal Mozart

This elegant dish is at home in either a sophisticated or rustic setting.

Hollandaise Sauce

4 egg yolks
2 tbsp. fresh lemon juice
1 tsp. white vinegar

¼ tsp. salt
2 drops Tabasco sauce
¾ cup butter

Veal

1½ lbs. veal cutlets
½ cup all-purpose
   flour
1½ tsp. salt
¼ tsp. freshly ground
   black pepper
2 eggs, beaten

¾ cup fine
   breadcrumbs
⅓ cup butter
12 stalks fresh or frozen
   asparagus, cooked
1 lb. mushrooms,
   sliced

In a blender or a food processor, blend egg yolks, lemon juice, vinegar, salt, and Tabasco for about 5 seconds. In a small pan, heat the butter until it foams. Then pour the butter into running blender or food processor in a steady stream. Turn off motor the moment mixture is creamy. Do not overblend. Set sauce aside.

Cut veal into 6 pieces and pound each piece until it is thin. On a plate, combine flour, salt, and pepper. Coat veal pieces with flour mixture. Dip each floured cutlet into beaten eggs, then dip into breadcrumbs. Set cutlets in refrigerator for 20 minutes to allow coating to set.

In a large skillet, melt the butter. Sauté cutlets over medium heat for 5 to 7 minutes, or until they are tender and well browned on both sides. Transfer cutlets to a warm serving platter. To the skillet, add sliced mushrooms; add another tablespoon of butter if necessary. Brown mushrooms lightly, then spoon some mushrooms onto each cutlet. Lay 2 asparagus spears on each cutlet. Coat cutlets with hollandaise sauce and place under a preheated broiler for 2 minutes, or until sauce is glazed. Serve at once.

Serves 6.

Gratinated Fruits

Fruit fulfilling its noblest aspirations.

Peel of 1 lemon
Peel of 1 orange
¼ cup orange juice
¼ cup lemon juice
½ cup butter
1 cup sugar
2 eggs
1 cup fresh straw-
  berries

1 cup fresh raspberries
1 cup fresh blueberries
1 banana
2 peaches
2 kiwi
8 tsp. sugar
8 tsp. kirsch
1 cup whipping (35%)
  cream

In a heavy saucepan over medium heat, combine lemon and orange peel, lemon and orange juice, butter, sugar, and eggs. Heat to the boiling point, stirring constantly. Remove from heat, remove lemon and orange peel, and let sauce cool.

While liquid is cooling, slice banana, peaches, and kiwi. (You should have about 1 cup of each. Place an equal amount of all fruits into eight individual ovenproof dessert dishes. Sprinkle each dish with 1 teaspoon sugar and 1 teaspoon kirsch. Warm the fruit cups in a 300°F oven.

While fruit cups are heating, whip cream until soft peaks form. Fold cream into cooled sauce. Pour an equal amount of sauce over each warm fruit cup, then place fruit cups under the broiler until sauce is golden brown.

Serves 8.

Steamed Apple-Bread Pudding

Light summer meals take well to a hearty dessert. You won't have to run to the store for these ingredients: they're found in most kitchens.

6 *large apples, peeled, cored, and finely chopped*	**1** *cup raisins*
	¾ *cup sugar*
	¼ *tsp. salt*
5 *eggs, beaten*	**Pinch ground nutmeg**
4 *cups breadcrumbs*	

In a large bowl, combine apples, eggs, breadcrumbs, raisins, sugar, salt, and nutmeg. Mix well. Pour batter into a well-greased 8-cup pudding mould. Cover tightly with lid or foil. In a large pot with a tight-fitting lid, set a rack. Place pudding on rack and pour in boiling water to half-way up the side of the mould. Set the pot on the stove. Cover and bring water to the boil. Simmer pudding for 3 hours, adding water to pot as needed.

Remove mould from pot, uncover, and unmould pudding onto serving plate.

This pudding is good with custard sauce or whipping cream.

Serves 8 to 10.

CHAPTER 4

CITY LIMITS

*Choose any direction and take a
relaxing drive away from urban activity.
In the Caledon Hills, see the mystique of the
trees: in spring, the maple-syrup harvest, and in the fall,
the panorama of colour as the leaves change with the
seasons. Antique shops, markets, roadside stands,
and delightful country restaurants offer
delicious day trips out of town.*

Recipes

Restaurants of the Region

APSLEY

Anderson Motel · Home cooking, Sunday roast, and fresh fruit pies

AURORA

La Faubourg · A casual, French country inn with exceptional food

Tailor House · Quaint and charming, this is a fastidious Dutch establishment

BRAMPTON

Chez Marie · In this mansion with six dining rooms, each named for a variety of rose, game and exotic dishes are featured

Via Veneto · Old-fashioned Italian cooking

CALEDON EAST

The Caledon Inn · British cuisine and pub lunches, homemade desserts

GEORGETOWN

Spot on 7 · Delicious home cooking

KING CITY

Hogan's Inn · A restored 1850s hotel, featuring continental cuisine

MAPLE

Auberge Maple Inn · French cuisine and fine formal dining

PICKERING

House Next Door · In an 1800 stucco cottage, homemade light meals, desserts, and an enormous variety of teas are served

TERRA COTTA

The Terra Cotta Inn · A grand antique-filled restaurant that serves classic cuisine and elegant afternoon tea

Maple-Syrup Icing

Seven-minute frosting with a maple-syrup bonus.

2 egg whites
1 cup maple syrup

Beat egg whites until soft peaks form. Set aside. In a
saucepan, boil maple syrup until it reaches the soft-ball stage.
(Drop ½ tsp. of the boiling syrup in cold water. Syrup is
ready when it forms a soft ball in the water.) Beat egg whites
again, gradually adding hot syrup. Beat until stiff and glossy
peaks form.

Makes 2 to 3 cups, or enough to ice a 9-inch layer cake.

Maple Sweet Potatoes

For about twenty-one days every spring, an old Indian social and
spiritual rite – called "Maple Moon" – takes place deep in the
Caledon Hills, the heart of the province's sugar bush. The ritual
involves tapping mature maple trees for syrup. And late at night,
when it's very still, the only sounds are the dripping of the sap into
buckets and the hissing of steam as water is boiled in the sugar shacks.

3 lbs. sweet potatoes	**2 tsp. grated orange**
½ cup maple syrup	**zest**
½ cup margarine or	**⅛ tsp. allspice**
butter	**½ tsp. salt**
1 cup apple juice	**Freshly ground pepper**

Scrub the sweet potatoes but do not peel. In a saucepan,
cover potatoes well with cold water. Bring water to a boil
and boil until potatoes are tender. Drain and peel.

In a ricer or a food mill, grind the sweet potatoes; place
ground potatoes in a large bowl. Add maple syrup,
margarine or butter, apple juice, orange zest, allspice, salt,
and pepper, and combine well. Spoon into a greased 2-quart
baking dish. Smooth the top with a rubber spatula, then
cover. Bake in a 350°F oven for 20 minutes, or until potatoes
are heated through. Serve hot.

Serves 8.

Note: This dish can be prepared in advance. Refrigerate potatoes in the covered baking dish until shortly before serving time. Bake in a 350°F oven for 30 minutes, or until potatoes are heated through.

Maple Mousse

Each maple tree gives up about two gallons of sap a day. It takes about forty-two gallons of sap to make one gallon of maple syrup. Enough to put spark into your sweet potatoes, glaze your roasts, pour over your pancakes, top your ice cream, sweeten your fruit, and put zing into a hot toddy. A gallon of maple syrup goes a long, long way.

1 ½ tbsp. unflavoured gelatin
½ cup cold water
2 cups maple syrup
8 egg yolks

¼ cup maple liqueur
1 tsp. vanilla
3 cups whipping (35%) cream

In a saucepan, sprinkle gelatin over cold water. Let stand for 5 minutes, then heat gently until gelatin is dissolved.

In a separate saucepan, bring maple syrup to a boil. In a large bowl, beat egg yolks well. Slowly pour hot syrup into eggs and whisk until smooth; then pour egg-syrup mixture back into the saucepan. Cook gently until custard is slightly thickened. Whisk in dissolved gelatin, then add maple liqueur and vanilla. Pour pudding into a large bowl and cool to room temperature.

Whip cream until firm. Put aside 1 ½ cups for garnish. Fold remainder into the custard. Spoon custard into a 9-inch spring-form pan and refrigerate for at least 6 hours. To serve, unmould mousse and serve chilled. Mousse looks elegant decorated with reserved whipped cream.

Serves 10 to 12.

Note: The mousse can also be frozen. Defrost it in the refrigerator before serving.

Stuffed Boneless Lamb Roast

The Caledon Hills offer grazing land, the perfect terrain for sheep and lamb. Spring lamb is always available for Easter.

1 boneless lamb shoulder

1 clove garlic, peeled and cut into slivers

2 cups breadcrumbs (made from fresh brown bread)

2 slices bacon, chopped

Grated rind of orange

1 egg

1 tsp. dried basil

1 tbsp. finely chopped fresh parsley

Juice of 1 orange

1 tbsp. honey

Open the lamb shoulder and spread it flat, skin-side down. Make small slits in the meat and insert garlic slivers.

In a large bowl, combine breadcrumbs, bacon, orange rind, egg, basil, and parsley. Spread lamb with stuffing. Roll meat up, tucking in any loose ends. Tie securely in several places with string.

On a rack in a roasting pan, roast shoulder in a 325°F oven for about 1 hour, or until meat is just pink. During the last 15 minutes of roasting, brush lamb with orange juice combined with honey.

Serves 4 to 6.

Ukrainian Meat Sticks

Old-country meat dishes may seem like a lot of work, but the results make the work worthwhile.

3 lbs. veal	½ tsp. curry powder
3 lbs. lean pork	Salt
6 cloves garlic	Pepper
¾ cup water	2 eggs
¼ cup wine vinegar	Oil
½ tsp. salt	2 medium onions,
¼ tsp. pepper	chopped
2 cups breadcrumbs	1 tbsp. butter, softened

Cut veal and pork into 1-inch cubes and place cubes in a large bowl. Chop garlic. In a small bowl, mix garlic, water, wine vinegar, salt, and pepper. Pour over meat cubes and stir. Marinate meat cubes for at least 3 hours, or overnight, to allow flavours to blend.

Leaving about 2 inches at the bottom of each skewer, arrange pork and veal cubes alternately on 6-inch wooden skewers. Squeeze cubes together. Continue to add meat until all the meat is used. You should fill 12 skewers.

In a shallow bowl, combine breadcrumbs, curry powder, salt, and pepper. In a second shallow bowl, beat eggs. Dip skewered meat cubes in breadcrumbs. Coat with egg, then dip in crumbs again.

In a large skillet, heat about 1 inch of cooking oil. Fry skewers of meat cubes, a few at a time, until meat is lightly browned. Combine onions and butter and spread in a large shallow baking dish. Place meat sticks on onions and bake in a 275°F oven for about 45 minutes, or until meat is no longer pink.

Serves 12.

Baked Stuffed Onions

Simcoe and York county farmers are proud of the produce they grow in the Bradford Marshes. Hardy and sweet carrots, onions, and other vegetables bring a fresh harvest taste to our dining tables during the winter months.

"There is in every cook's opinion no savoury dish without an onion." – Anonymous

4 medium-sized yellow cooking onions
2 slices day-old bread
¼ tsp. ground sage
¼ tsp. ground savory
¼ tsp. dried thyme leaves
¼ tsp. paprika
¼ tsp. salt
3 tbsp. melted butter
¼ cup grated Cheddar cheese

Cut off ends of onions and peel. Place in a saucepan and cover with boiling water. Boil rapidly, uncovered, for 15 minutes.

While onions are cooking, break bread into coarse crumbs and place in a mixing bowl.

When onions are cooked, drain and allow to cool slightly. Cut in half crosswise and remove centres, leaving shells two or three layers thick. Set shells aside. Chop centres coarsely and add to breadcrumbs. Add sage, savory, thyme, paprika, salt, and melted butter, and mix. Spoon mixture into onion shells, then sprinkle with grated Cheddar. Place in a greased shallow baking dish, cover, and bake in a 350°F oven for 35 to 40 minutes, or until golden brown.

Very nice garnish for a roast.

Serves 4.

Scotch Graham Scones

Country cooking means a hearty breakfast. Just the right fuel to keep you going for a morning of cross-country skiing in the Caledon Hills.

1 cup all-purpose flour	⅓ cup sugar
2 tsp. baking powder	½ cup shortening
½ tsp. salt	1 egg
1 cup graham flour	Water

In a large mixing bowl, sift together all-purpose flour, baking powder, and salt. Stir in graham flour and sugar. Cut in shortening until mixture is crumbly.

Break egg into a measuring cup and beat with a fork. To measuring cup, add water until there is ⅔ cup liquid. Remove 1 tbsp. egg and pour it into a saucer; set aside. With a fork, stir egg and water into flour mixture to make a soft, slightly sticky dough.

Turn dough out on a lightly floured surface and knead gently 8 or 10 times. Roll out dough until it forms a large circle about a half-inch thick. Cut circle into 8 wedges. Brush each wedge with reserved egg and set on an ungreased cookie sheet. Bake in a 450°F oven for 12 to 15 minutes, until wedges are a light golden-brown. Serve warm.

These scones are delicious with butter and jam.

Makes 8 scones.

Welsh Cakes

After a hike in the Caledon Hills, this tasty treat will hit the spot.

2 cups all-purpose flour
3 tbsp. sugar
¼ tsp. baking powder
½ cup butter
½ cup currants
2 eggs, beaten
Sugar for sprinkling

In a large bowl, combine flour, sugar, and baking powder. Cut in the butter until mixture is crumbly. Stir in currants. Add beaten eggs and beat until mixture forms a stiff dough.

On a lightly floured surface, roll out dough to one-quarter inch thick. With a floured cookie cutter, cut dough into 3-inch rounds. Set cakes on a lightly greased hot griddle. When bottoms are golden brown, turn and cook other side. When second side is done, turn griddle off. Leave cakes on griddle for a few moments to dry them slightly. While still warm, sprinkle cakes with sugar.

Makes 10 to 12 cakes.

Carrot Jam

Summer sunshine on toast.

10 carrots
3 cups sugar
½ tsp. ground ginger
Rind of 1 lemon
Juice of 1 lemon
1 tbsp. brandy
(optional)

Peel carrots and cut into thin slices. Cook in boiling water for 12 to 15 minutes, or until tender. Drain. In a blender or a food processor, purée carrots.

In a large saucepan or preserving kettle, combine carrot purée, sugar, ginger, lemon rind, and lemon juice; mix thoroughly. Bring slowly to the boil, stirring constantly until sugar dissolves. Reduce heat; cook, uncovered, for about 20 minutes, or until jam sets when a spoonful is placed on a cold saucer. Add brandy if desired. Ladle into hot sterilized jars; seal with melted wax or self-sealing lids.

Makes about five 8-ounce jars.

Swiss-Style Celeriac Salad

An unusual, crunchy, and sophisticated buffet item.

1 cup mayonnaise
2 tbsp. whipping (35%) cream
1 heaping tsp. German mustard
1 tbsp. apple-cider vinegar
1 tsp. salt

4 large celeriac nobs, peeled and coarsely grated
1 Granny Smith apple, peeled, cored, and coarsely grated
½ cup coarsely chopped hazelnuts, toasted

In a large mixing bowl, combine mayonnaise, cream, mustard, vinegar, and salt. Add celeriac and apple and toss well. Stir in toasted hazelnuts. Cover and chill for 2 hours, to allow flavours to blend.

Salad is good served heaped onto a bed of watercress and sprinkled with toasted hazelnuts.

Serves 6.

Dill-Pickle and Sour-Cream Soup

Yes, it tastes delicious!

3 tbsp. butter
⅓ cup chopped onion
½ cup dry white wine
⅓ cup plus 1 tbsp.
  all-purpose flour
5 cups water
1½ cups juice from
  pickle jar, strained
4 large crisp dill
  pickles, diced

2 tsp. dried dill or
  4 tsp. fresh dill
½ cup sour cream
⅛ tsp. poultry seasoning
Salt
⅛ tsp. white pepper
Diced pickle
  (for garnish)

In a large pot or Dutch oven over medium heat, melt the butter. Add onion and sauté until onion is soft. Add wine and continue to cook until almost all liquid has evaporated. Reduce heat to low and stir in flour. Be careful not to let it brown. In a separate bowl, combine water and pickle juice, then whisk into onion and wine all at once. Increase heat and bring to a boil, stirring constantly, until soup thickens. Add diced pickles and dill. Chill well. Before serving, stir in sour cream. Add poultry seasoning, salt, and pepper. If desired, garnish each serving with diced pickle.

Serves 8.

Swiss Corn-and-Pepper Salad

A quick and colourful hearty dish that knows no seasons.

1 7-oz. can whole-
  kernel corn,
  drained
1 4-oz. jar sliced
  pimiento, drained

1 red bell pepper,
  seeded and
  chopped
½ cup grated Swiss
  cheese

¼ *cup minced fresh*	**10** *cherry tomatoes*
parsley	**7** *tbsp. olive oil*
1 *small bunch green*	**2** *tbsp. wine vinegar*
onions, chopped	¼ *tsp. dried tarragon*
1 *green pepper, seeded*	¼ *tsp. dry mustard*
and chopped	¼ *tsp. salt*
	Freshly ground pepper

To make salad: In a large glass bowl, combine corn, pimiento, parsley, onions, green and red pepper, cheese, and cherry tomatoes.

To make dressing: Place olive oil, vinegar, tarragon, mustard, salt, and pepper in bowl or a jar with a tight-fitting lid. Whisk or shake until thoroughly blended. Pour over salad and toss well. Serve chilled.

Serves 6.

Green-Peas and Bacon Salad

A salad with fixings from the refrigerator can be as tasty as one with garden-fresh veggies.

1 *cup yogurt*	¼ *cup minced red*
1 *tsp. seasoned salt*	*onion*
¼ *tsp. lemon pepper*	½ *lb. bacon, cooked,*
¼ *tsp. minced garlic*	*drained, and*
3 *cups frozen peas,*	*crumbled*
thawed	**1** *small tomato, diced*

In a medium-sized bowl, combine yogurt, salt, pepper, and garlic. Add peas and onion. Mix thoroughly and chill for several hours or overnight. At serving time, add tomato and bacon and toss lightly.

Serves 6.

Roasted-Pepper and Dandelion Salad

Before the dandelion's yellow flowers light up your lawn, pluck the tender leaves and make this salad. It will light up your table.

4 large red peppers	**Salt**
6 tbsp. olive oil	**Freshly ground pepper**
3 to 4 tbsp. red wine	**5 cups young dandelion**
vinegar	**greens**
	½ small red onion, thinly sliced

Roast peppers over a hot fire or under the broiler until charred on all sides. Transfer the peppers to a paper bag. Close the bag tightly and let stand for about 1 hour. Remove peppers from the bag and peel off skins; discard skins, stems, and seeds. Slice peppers into thin strips.

In a large bowl, stir together olive oil, vinegar, salt, and pepper. Add dandelion greens and onion and toss; add peppers and toss again.

Serves 6 to 8.

Note: Escarole can be substituted for dandelion greens.

Green-Bean, Almond, and Feta-Cheese Salad

An intriguing combination, this salad can be served as a first course.

1½ lbs. fresh green	**¾ tsp. salt**
beans	**½ tsp. minced garlic**
¾ cup olive oil	**¼ tsp. freshly ground**
½ cup packed fresh	**pepper**
mint leaves,	**1 cup chopped toasted**
chopped	**almonds**
¼ cup wine	**1 cup diced red onion**
vinegar	**1 cup crumbled feta**
	cheese

Trim ends of beans and cut beans in half. In boiling salted water, cook beans just until crisp. Drain beans well, and immediately plunge into ice water to stop cooking. Drain beans again; pat dry with paper towels.

In a blender, combine olive oil, mint leaves, vinegar, salt, garlic, and pepper. Blend well.

In a shallow glass serving bowl, arrange beans. Sprinkle with walnuts, onion, and cheese. Just before serving, pour dressing over salad and toss thoroughly.

Serves 6.

Note: This salad is also good made with Parmesan cheese. Use 1 cup of grated Parmesan instead of the feta cheese.

Turkish Vegetable Salad

Bored with leafy green salads? Experience this eastern mélange.

½ lb. small whole mushrooms	12 cherry tomatoes
1 19-oz. can chick peas, drained	1 cup yogurt
1 cup black olives	½ cup mayonnaise
¾ cup coarsely chopped green onion	2 garlic cloves, mashed
2 green peppers, chopped	2 tbsp. olive oil
2 red peppers, chopped	1 tbsp. lemon juice
	1 tsp. powdered cumin
	⅛ tsp. turmeric
	Salt
	Freshly ground pepper
	Lettuce leaves

In a saucepan, cook mushrooms in boiling water for 2 minutes. Drain and cool.

In a large bowl, combine chick peas, olives, green onion, green and red peppers, and tomatoes. Add cooked mushrooms and chill for 2 hours.

In a small bowl, mix yogurt, mayonnaise, garlic, olive oil, lemon juice, cumin, turmeric, salt, and pepper. Chill for 2 hours. Just before serving, pour dressing over salad and toss lightly. Serve on lettuce leaves.

Serves 6.

Dutch Cheese and Shrimp Puffs

These puffs make a tasty cocktail snack or light lunch.

½ cup butter	½ cup tiny shrimp
1 cup water	1 tbsp. chopped onion
1 ¾ cups all-purpose flour	Salt
6 eggs	Pepper
2 cups shredded Gouda	Dash of Tabasco
or Edam cheese	Oil for deep frying

In a saucepan, bring butter and water to a boil. Add flour and stir vigorously with a wooden spoon until batter leaves the sides of the saucepan. Remove from heat and allow batter to cool to room temperature. (If it is not cool enough, the eggs will cook in the batter.) Add eggs one at a time, beating well after each addition. Stir in cheese, shrimp, onion, salt, pepper, and Tabasco.

In a deep frying pan, pour 2 inches of cooking oil. Heat oil to 375°F. Drop batter into hot oil by the spoonful. (You can fry about 12 puffs at a time.) Fry puffs until they are golden. Remove with a slotted spoon and drain on paper towels. Serve warm in a napkin-lined dish. Puffs can be kept hot in a warm oven.

Makes 4 to 5 dozen puffs.

🌿 Brandy Snaps

A Victorian-era tea dainty that is making a fashionable come-back.

¼ cup butter	1 tsp. brandy
4 tbsp. light corn syrup	½ tsp. ground ginger
6 tbsp. sugar	1 cup whipping (35%) cream (optional)
½ cup all-purpose flour	

In the top half of a double boiler over low heat, melt butter, corn syrup, and sugar, stirring constantly until liquid is smooth. Remove from heat and stir in the flour, brandy, and ginger. Continue to stir until liquid is smooth.

On a well-greased baking sheet, drop rounded teaspoons of the batter about 4 inches apart. You should have only 4 or 5 snaps on each cookie sheet. Bake in a 300°F oven for 6 to 8 minutes, or until the snaps spread into circles and turn golden brown.

Allow the snaps to cool slightly, then loosen them from the baking sheet with a knife or spatula. Working quickly, place a snap in the palm of your hand, then wrap around the greased handle of a wooden spoon to form a cylinder. Hold in place until set, then slide the snap onto a rack to cool. Repeat until all snaps are cooked and rolled. If the snaps become too stiff to roll, set them back on the baking sheet and warm them briefly in the oven.

Makes 18 to 20 snaps.

Note: When snaps are completely cool, they can be filled. Whip the cream until stiff, then fill each snap with cream.

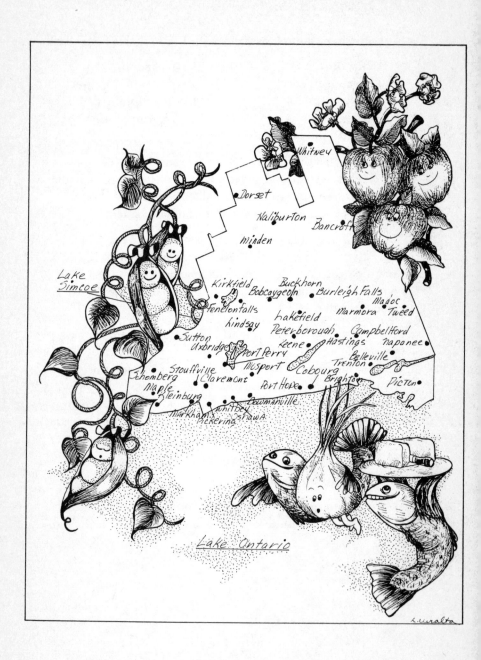

Whitney

Dorset

Haliburton   Bancroft

minden

Lake
Simcoe

Kirkfield   Buckhorn
Bobcaygeon   Burleigh Falls
Fenelonfalls   Madoc
                    Marmora   Tweed
Lindsay   Lakefield
         Peterborough   Campbelford
Sutton   napanee
Uxbridge   Keene   Hastings
         Port Perry
                    Belleville
Stouffville   Mosport   Trenton
Schomberg   Claremont   Cobourg
Maple   Brighton   Picton
Kleinburg   Port Hope
                    Bowmanville
Markham   Whitby
Pickering   Oshawa

Lake Ontario

L.uralta

120

CHAPTER 5

MIDDLE
OF THE ROAD

*Sand dunes, beaches, and some of
the finest fresh-water fishing imaginable
await in the centre of the province. Pretty towns
echo with the history of the United Empire Loyalists whose
traditions remain strong. Cruise along the Trent-Severn
canal system and stop for a proper English tea, a bed-and-
breakfast, a dinner at an inn, or a picnic in picturesque
surroundings.*

Recipes

Restaurants of the Region

BANCROFT

Esmond's Tea Room • The place for homemade butter tarts, bouncy piano tunes, and a personal style of hospitality

River Bend Motor Inn • Modern facilities with a pleasant dining room and cafeteria

BELLEVILLE

Dinkles • Like a scene right out of Dickens, with Windsor chairs, oak panelling, and a hearty menu

The Limestone Café • A light and pleasing menu in a warm limestone interior

BRIGHTON

The Galley • An airy Marina restaurant that serves schnitzels and seafood

COBOURG

The Dressler House • A charming brick cottage, restored with Victoriana. A lovely place to dine

Northumberland Heights Country Inn • Mostly schnitzel in a setting reminiscent of the Rhineland

The Rendezvous • Excellent food and an international menu

Seasons • Seasonal foods and baking to eat in or take out

CONSECON

The Sword • Olde English style and a large menu

GORE'S LANDING

Victoria Inn • Beautiful old home with two dining rooms

GRAFTON

St. Anne's Castle • Bed and breakfast in a beautifully restored, rambling, turreted castle

JACKSON'S POINT

The Briar's Resort • Continental cuisine is offered in the dining room

ORONO

The New Dutch Oven • Hearty buffets at lunch and dinner

OSHAWA

Parkwood Estate • "What's good for General Motors is good for the country." This magnificent estate was built for Colonel R. S. McLaughlin in the early 1900s. Luncheon and tea is served and there is an art gallery and greenhouse complex to tour

PICTON

Villeneuve Castle • This 180-year-old castle, complete with a ghost, shows its age but the owner/chef serves a good meal

The Waring House • A 150-year-old mansion preserved and filled with Canadiana

PORT PERRY

The Murray House • Excellent continental menu

ROSEMONT

The Globe • In the early days, Rosemont boasted four hotels, one of which was the Globe. The Needles family owns the Globe today, and if William Needles isn't always there, he may be appearing on Broadway, at Stratford, or another of all the world's "stages"

UXBRIDGE

The Hobby Horse Arms • A touch of English Essex County. Here you can find a cheerful Whitbread Trophy Bitters and Watneys Red Barrel on draft, Melton Mowbray Pie, Cornish pasties, hot crumbly cheese scones, and beef fondues

VIOLET HILL

Mrs. Mitchell's • A country restaurant that city people love. The ninety-seven-year-old one-room schoolhouse is the setting for some of the tastiest country recipes around

Garlic Mayonnaise

Garlic is as ancient as history itself. The Greeks made offerings of garlic cloves to the Goddess of the Occult; centuries later, people carried garlic to drive away evil spirits. Buddhists and Hindus condemned garlic for distracting men's thoughts from the celestial plane to earthly delights. Moslems believed that garlic plants sprang up in the left footprint of Satan when he was ejected from Islam's Eden. Moses taught that garlic gave strength to the Jewish people, and it is recommended by Ezra in the Talmud. The Anglo-Saxons had a hand in the spunky herb's history, too: they named it *gar* ("lance-shaped") *leac* ("plant").

6 *cloves garlic, peeled*
1 *tsp. salt*
2 *egg yolks*
1½ *cups olive oil*

1 *tbsp. hot water*
Freshly ground pepper
Lemon juice

Have all ingredients at room temperature.

Using a mortar and pestle, pound garlic and ½ tsp. of the salt together to make a paste. Transfer to a bowl and stir in egg yolks. Slowly whisk in oil, at first drop by drop, then in a steady stream. Beat in hot water to stabilize and lighten sauce. Adjust flavour with remaining ½ tsp. salt; add pepper and lemon juice to taste. Serve at room temperature.

Makes about 2 cups.

Note: This sauce is also good made with corn oil. Use ¾ cup olive oil and ¾ cup corn oil. The sauce can be refrigerated, but do not stir it when you take it out of the refrigerator. Let stand until it reaches room temperature before serving.

How to Handle Freshly Caught Fish

Fish will keep on ice for two or three days, but the flavour deteriorates as time goes by.

To gut: split the underside from vent to gills and remove innards. Discard the innards and wash the fish well.

To gill: remove pelvic fins by cutting around the muscle and dorsal by cutting against the fin.

To scale: use the blunt side of a heavy kitchen knife, or use a commercial scaler. Grasp the tail and run the knife from tail to head. This is best done underwater, because the scales tend to fly around.

To fillet: use a sharp, flexible knife. Remove head, then cut along the spine from head end to tail. Insert the knife blade under the cut you have made and scrape flesh off the rib cage. Cut as close to the bones as possible.

Crispy-Skin Barbecued Trout

In spring, trout can be seen in the brooks and streams in conservation areas. At Rice Lake, the fisher is almost assured of a good day's catch.

1 large trout, about 2½ lbs.	2 tbsp. vegetable oil
1 lemon, cut in half	1 tsp. curry powder
½ cup soy sauce	½ tsp. powdered ginger
2 tbsp. sugar	⅓ cup chopped green onion
2 tbsp. lemon juice	Flour for dredging

Clean fish, leaving head and tail intact. Rub inside and out with cut lemon.

In a bowl, combine soy sauce, sugar, lemon juice, oil, curry powder, ginger, and green onion. Place fish in bowl and marinate for 1 hour. Remove fish from marinade. Pat fish dry, dip in flour, then dip in marinade again. Place in a well-greased hinged fish basket. Place basket on grill over medium-hot coals and barbecue trout for 10 minutes per inch of thickness. Turn trout once or twice during barbecuing. Remove fish from basket to serving platter and serve immediately.

Serves 4 to 6.

Sweet-and-Sour Lake Simcoe Trout

Trout from the icy waters of Lake Simcoe take well to any cooking method.

2 lbs. lake trout, cut into serving-sized pieces
2 tbsp. butter
½ cup minced onion
1½ cups apple juice
½ cup apple-cider vinegar
⅔ cup firmly packed light-brown sugar
½ cup seedless raisins
2 bay leaves
1 tsp. salt
½ cup crushed ginger-snap cookies

Rinse fish. In a large skillet, melt the butter. Add onion and cook until soft but not brown. Stir in apple juice, vinegar, brown sugar, raisins, bay leaves, and salt. Heat to boiling; simmer for 5 minutes to blend flavours.

Add fillets, cover, and simmer for 3 to 5 minutes, or until fish flakes easily when tested with a fork. Remove fish from liquid and place it in a serving dish. Cover to keep warm.

Remove bay leaves from liquid and discard. To liquid in frying pan, gradually add crushed ginger snaps, stirring until sauce is smooth and thickened. Pour sauce over fish and serve immediately.

Serves 6.

Pan-Fried Trout
with Hazelnuts and Grapes

"Summertime, and the living is easy Fish are jumpin' . . ." That line could well apply to the activity at Lake Simcoe, Rice Lake, and all the other fertile fishing spots in the area. During the long fishing season, a mess of trout is a common meal.

6 small trout, filleted (12 fillets)	**2 tbsp. whipping (35%) cream**
Salt	**1 cup milk**
Pepper	**¾ cup butter**
1 cup all-purpose flour, sifted	**¼ cup chopped hazelnuts**
½ tsp. salt	**1 cup seedless green grapes**
2 eggs, beaten	

Rinse trout fillets under cold water. Pat dry and season with salt and pepper.

Sift together flour and salt. In a separate bowl, beat together eggs, cream, and milk. Add flour to egg mixture and stir until batter is smooth.

In a large saucepan, heat ½ cup of the butter. Dip trout in batter, then pan-fry on both sides until flesh is opaque and flakes easily. (Allow 10 to 12 minutes per inch of thickness.) Lift trout from pan and set on a platter, cover, and keep warm.

In the same frying pan, sauté hazelnuts until light brown. Add grapes and heat thoroughly. Stir in remaining ¼ cup butter. Spoon sauce over trout and serve immediately.

Serves 6.

Whole Baked Trout with Red Peppers

1 whole trout, about
    4 lbs., cleaned
    and dressed,
    head on
2 cloves garlic, peeled
    and cut in half
1 lime, sliced
Sprigs of fresh
    parsley, tarragon,
    and marjoram
Salt
Freshly ground pepper

2 tbsp. butter
½ cup dry vermouth
2 tbsp. olive oil
1 medium onion,
    minced
4 red peppers, peeled,
    seeded, and
    sliced
1 tbsp. finely chopped
    parsley
Juice of 1 lime

Rinse fish and pat dry. Place in a lightly buttered baking dish. Make three or four diagonal incisions through the skin along one side of the trout. Insert half a garlic clove and a thin slice of lime into each slit. Scatter sprigs of parsley, tarragon, and marjoram over trout. Sprinkle with salt and pepper. Dot fish with butter and pour vermouth over top. Measure fish at its thickest point; cover baking dish with buttered foil and bake in a 450°F oven for 10 minutes for each inch of thickness.

In a large frying pan, heat olive oil. Add onion and remaining garlic and cook for 5 to 7 minutes, or until onion is soft. Stir in peppers and cook until heated through. Add parsley; add lime juice and salt to taste.

When fish is cooked, place on a heated platter, reserving cooking juices. With a slotted spoon, remove garlic and peppers from frying pan and set aside. To the frying pan, add reserved fish-cooking juices. Place frying pan over medium heat and reduce juices to ½ cup. Pour liquid over fish. Garnish with pepper.

Serves 4 to 6.

Steak and Kidney Pie

In the early 1800s, Scottish and German immigrants settled in the village of Uxbridge. The community retains its roots: steak and kidney pie, Scottish shortbread, and many kinds of scones are served in restaurants. From Whitney to Trenton, from Belleville to Barry's Bay, the towns in this area hold pleasant surprises for the day-tripper or weekend visitor. One thing you can be sure of: you will always eat well.

¾ lb. calves' kidney	1 cup beef stock
2 tbsp. all-purpose flour	1 bay leaf
	1 tsp. chopped parsley
1 tsp. salt	Pinch powdered cloves
¾ tsp. black pepper	Pinch marjoram
2 lbs. round steak, cut into bite-sized pieces	Flaky Pastry (see page 131)
4 tbsp. butter	1 tbsp. dry sherry
4 shallots, finely chopped	1 tsp. Worcestershire sauce

Clean kidney. Cut in half lengthwise, and remove fat and large tubes. Place kidney in a bowl and cover with salted water. Soak kidney for 1 hour. Dry kidney and cut into quarter-inch-thick slices.

In a small bowl, combine flour, salt, and ½ teaspoon of the pepper. Dredge steak pieces and kidney slices in the seasoned flour; make sure each piece is well coated.

In a thick-bottomed saucepan, melt the butter. Sauté shallots until golden. Add the beef and kidney pieces. Cook, stirring constantly, until meat is brown. Stir in beef stock, remaining ¼ teaspoon pepper, bay leaf, chopped parsley, powdered cloves, and marjoram. Bring stock to a boil; cover and simmer over low heat for 1 to 1½ hours or until meat is tender.

Grease a deep baking dish. Place a pie funnel in the centre of the dish; pour meat and liquid around funnel and allow to cool. While meat is cooling, roll out pastry crust. Place pastry over baking dish. Moisten the edge of the crust and pinch it to the dish to seal. Make sure that pie funnel has pierced crust to allow steam to escape. Bake in a 450°F oven for 10 minutes, then lower heat to 375°F and bake for 15 more minutes, or until crust is golden brown.

Combine sherry and Worcestershire sauce. Just before serving the pie, remove funnel and pour in sherry mixture.

Serves 6.

Flaky Pastry

¼ cup butter
½ cup vegetable
    shortening
1 ¾ cups all-purpose
    flour

1 tsp. salt
6 tbsp. ice water
2 tbsp. white vinegar

Cut butter and shortening into small pieces. In a large bowl, sift together flour and salt. Add butter and shortening. Rub together lightly with fingers. All at once pour in water and vinegar. Mix and form into a ball.

On a floured pastry board, knead pastry lightly and roll into a rectangle. Fold and knead again. Chill 10 minutes. Roll once more and knead. Chill until ready to use.

Aunt Isa's Scottish Shortbread

Auntie's legacy to four generations of her family. A Christmas tradition.

1 lb. unsalted butter, at room temperature	Yolk of 1 egg
	¼ cup rice flour
	6 cups sifted cake-and-pastry flour
1 cup sugar	

In a large bowl, cream together butter and sugar. Blend in egg yolk. In a separate bowl, combine rice and pastry flours. Add flours to creamed mixture and stir until mixed. Turn dough onto a lightly floured surface. Knead dough thoroughly. (It will take about 7 minutes.)

Roll out half the dough until it is one-quarter inch thick. Prick lightly all over with a fork. With a sharp knife, cut dough into rectangular or diamond shapes. Repeat for second half of dough.

Set shapes on ungreased cookie sheets and bake in a 325°F oven for 15 to 20 minutes, or until barely golden. Remove from oven and leave on cookie sheets to cool.

Makes 4 to 5 dozen shortbread.

Philippine Poppy-Seed Cake

Settlers from foreign lands enrich the culinary scene.

½ cup poppy seeds	¼ cup rum
1 cup milk	1 cup chopped walnuts
2 cups sugar	2 cups all-purpose flour
1¼ cups vegetable oil	2 tsp. baking powder
6 eggs	¼ tsp. salt

In a small bowl, combine poppy seeds and ½ cup of the milk and allow to soak for 10 minutes; drain. While seeds are soaking, in a large bowl, beat together sugar and oil. Add eggs one at a time, beating well after each addition.

In a separate bowl, stir rum into remaining ½ cup milk. Stir into sugar-egg mixture. Add walnuts and drained poppy seeds. Stir in flour, baking powder, and salt. Pour batter into a greased 10-inch tube or Bundt pan. Bake in a 350°F oven for 1 hour, or until a toothpick inserted in the centre of the cake comes out clean.

Makes one 10-inch cake.

Rhubarb Cake

Rhubarb adds tang to this simple-to-make summer coffee cake. Whether your rhubarb patch is in Leaside or in the Kawarthas, this recipe will be a *coup*. It never fails.

½ cup shortening	1 tsp. vanilla
1½ cups brown sugar	1½ cups chopped
1 egg	rhubarb
2 cups all-purpose flour	⅓ cup white sugar
1 tsp. baking soda	1 tsp. cinnamon
1 cup buttermilk	

In a large bowl, cream together shortening and brown sugar. Add egg and beat well.

Combine flour and baking soda. In a separate bowl, combine buttermilk and vanilla. Stir flour mixture into sugar and egg alternately with buttermilk mixture. Fold in rhubarb.

In a small bowl, stir together sugar and cinnamon for topping. Pour batter into a greased 9 by 13-inch pan and sprinkle top with sugar-cinnamon mixture. Bake in a 350°F oven for 40 to 50 minutes, or until a toothpick inserted in centre of cake comes out clean.

Serves 10 to 12.

Note: No buttermilk? Add 1 tbsp. vinegar to 1 cup of milk; let stand for 5 minutes, until milk is curdled, then use as you would buttermilk.

English Mixed Grill

The United Empire Loyalists, were comprised of immigrants from many parts of the British Isles, united by one common cause – loyalty to the British Crown. This recipe is a combination that also works well together.

2 large or 4 small
    sausage links
4 thick slices Canadian
    bacon
Vegetable oil
Salt
Freshly ground pepper
2 3-oz. boneless sirloin
    steaks or filet
    mignons
2 lamb chops

2 3-oz. pieces calf's
    liver
2 lamb kidneys (2 to
    3 oz. each), rinsed
    and split,
    membrane and
    fat removed
2 medium-fresh ripe
    tomatoes, halved
2 large mushroom caps
Chopped fresh parsley
Dried oregano

Before starting, have all ingredients at room temperature. Warm two dinner plates. Preheat broiler.

Prick sausage lightly in several places with a fork and place sausage and bacon on a well-oiled broiler pan. Broil 4 to 6 inches from source of heat for 4 to 5 minutes, or until sausage and bacon are browned on one side. Turn sausage and bacon; cook on second side for about 2 minutes. Transfer bacon to ovenproof plates; and keep warm. Cook sausage 2 to 3 minutes longer. Remove sausage from pan; add to plates with bacon.

Place steaks and lamb chops on the broiler pan and brush meat with oil. Broil 3 to 4 minutes, then sprinkle with salt and pepper to taste. Turn and brush second side lightly with oil. Broil 2 to 3 minutes on second side; remove from pan. Sprinkle with salt and pepper. Add to plates with sausage and bacon.

Add calf's liver and lamb kidneys to broiler pan; brush lightly with oil. Broil liver and kidney about 3 minutes on the first side. Turn, brush second side lightly with oil, and broil for about 2 minutes; remove from pan. Sprinkle with salt and pepper. Add to plates.

Add tomatoes and mushroom caps to broiler pan; brush with oil. Sprinkle with salt, pepper, and parsley to taste; sprinkle tomatoes with oregano. Cook 2 to 3 minutes. Remove from pan and add to plates.

Serve immediately with a variety of mustards: sweet, hot, and brown.

Serves 2.

Spinach Dip

Don't tell them what's in it. There won't be a scrap left of this zesty mix.

1 10-oz. package chopped frozen spinach
1 cup sour cream
1 cup mayonnaise
1 package Knorr vegetable-soup mix

1 8-oz. can water chestnuts, drained and chopped
4 tbsp. chopped onion

In a blender or a food processor, blend spinach, sour cream, and mayonnaise until mixture is smooth. Add soup mix, water chestnuts, and onion. Blend just until mixed through. Let stand for 2 hours before serving, to allow flavours to blend.

To serve, pour into a round, hollowed-out loaf of white or pumpernickel bread. Cut up the bread you removed from the loaf into bite-sized pieces for dipping in the spinach dip.

Makes 4 cups.

Note: The dip can be made with fresh spinach. Use half a package of fresh spinach; rinse leaves well and chop finely.

Duck Pâté

Actress Marie Dressler, best known for her role as "Tug Boat Annie," grew up in a little cottage, which has been restored and houses one of Cobourg's finest restaurants. A specialty of the house is this duck pâté, adapted here for the home kitchen.

½ lb. thinly sliced barding fat (pork back fat)	1½ tsp. salt
	1 tsp. ground white pepper
1 duck (4 lbs.)	¼ cup whipping (35%) cream
¾ lb. pork back fat, cubed	
2 eggs	¼ lb. unsalted cashew nuts, toasted
1 tbsp. all-purpose flour	1 10-oz. can condensed chicken broth

Line a 5-cup mould with slices of barding fat. Cut enough meat from the duck to make 1 pound. Cut a quarter of the duck meat into cubes and set aside. In a food processor, combine remaining duck with cubed barding fat and chop coarsely by turning the food processor on and off in short bursts.

Pour three-quarters of the chopped mixture into a large bowl and set aside.

To remaining mixture in food processor, add eggs, flour, salt, and pepper. Process till creamy. Add to chopped mixture in the large bowl. To the large bowl, also add the cream, cashews, reserved cubed duck meat, and chicken broth. Blend well.

With a spoon, pack mixture into the mould. Bang the mould on the counter to remove any air pockets. Cover tightly with aluminum foil. Place mould in a large shallow pan and pour boiling water into the pan so that it reaches half-way up the mould. Bake in a 350°F oven for about 1 hour and 30 minutes, or until firm and set. Cool slightly, then refrigerate overnight. Unmould and slice to serve.

Serves 8 to 10.

Note: Foil may be removed during last half hour of baking, to allow pâté to brown.

The duck carcass can be used to make soup.

Saxe-Coburg Soup

The charming town of Cobourg, on Lake Ontario, has visitors all year round. It's a lovely place to spend the day. In 1819, to honour the marriage of Princess Charlotte to Prince Leopold of Saxe-Coburg, the town, originally called Amhurst, changed its name to Cobourg.

2 tbsp. butter
1 medium onion, finely
   chopped
2 medium potatoes,
   peeled and diced
4 cups chicken stock
1 tbsp. sugar
1 lb. Brussels sprouts,
   trimmed, outer
   leaves removed

1½ cups table (18%)
   cream
⅛ lb. cooked ham,
   finely diced
½ cup dry sherry
Salt
Freshly ground black
   pepper

In a soup pot, melt the butter. Add the onion and sauté gently until the onion is soft but not brown. Add the potatoes, stock, sugar, and Brussels sprouts. Bring the stock to a boil, then lower the heat, cover, and simmer for about 15 minutes, or until the sprouts and potatoes are tender.

Pour the soup into a blender or food processor and purée, then return soup to the saucepan. Stir in the cream, ham, and sherry, and season to taste with salt and pepper. Heat soup gently but do not let it boil. This soup is also good served cold.

Serves 6.

Note: If Brussels sprouts are out of season, substitute a 10-oz. package of frozen sprouts for the fresh ones.

Quick Onion-Cheese Biscuits

The rush to find gold in Eldorado in 1866 was so vibrant that sixteen hotels were built to accommodate the influx of prospectors. Today the population is forty-eight–but the gold still exists. Eldorado gold is a mellow yellow Cheddar. It makes an ideal treat for Sunday-morning brunch.

2½ cups all-purpose flour	1 cup shredded extra-old Cheddar cheese
3 tsp. baking powder	1 large onion
¼ tsp. salt	2 tbsp. butter
½ cup margarine or butter	1 egg, beaten
	¾ cup milk

Sift together flour, baking powder, and salt. With a pastry blender or two knives, cut butter into flour mixture. Stir in shredded cheese.

Slice onion in thin rounds, then cut slices in half. In a skillet, brown onion in butter. Add onion to flour-butter mixture. Add beaten egg and milk. Drop heaping tablespoons of dough in a circle on a greased cookie sheet. The mounds of dough should just touch each other.

Bake in a 400°F oven for approximately 20 to 25 minutes, or until biscuits are golden brown.

Makes 1 ring of biscuits.

🖋 Cinnamon-Walnut Coffee Cake

It takes just a few moments to put this coffee cake together. At the gorgeous St. Anne's Castle in Grafton, it is made fresh every morning for bed-and-breakfast guests.

½ cup walnuts	2 eggs
1 ½ cups sugar	1 cup sour cream
1 tbsp. cinnamon	1 ½ cups all-purpose flour
½ cup cold butter, cut into 4 pieces	1 ½ tsp. baking powder
	1 tsp. baking soda
1 tsp. vanilla	⅛ tsp. salt

In a food processor fitted with a metal blade, place walnuts, ½ cup of the sugar, and cinnamon. Process, turning on and off, until mixture is combined and nuts are coarsely chopped. Pour cinnamon-walnut mixture into a small bowl and set aside.

In the food processor, still with the metal blade, place butter, remaining 1 cup of sugar, and vanilla. Process until all ingredients are combined, about 30 seconds. Add eggs and sour cream and process for about 1 minute, or until thoroughly mixed.

In a mixing bowl, combine flour, baking powder, baking soda, and salt. Stir to mix, then add to butter-sugar mixture. Turn food processor on and off three or four times, or until flour is absorbed.

Butter and flour a 9-cup tube pan or an 8-inch spring-form pan. Place half the batter in the pan; top with half the cinnamon-walnut mixture. Add remaining batter and sprinkle top evenly with remaining cinnamon-walnut mixture. Bake in a 350°F oven for 45 to 50 minutes, or until toothpick inserted in the centre comes out clean. Cool on a wire rack.

Makes 1 cake.

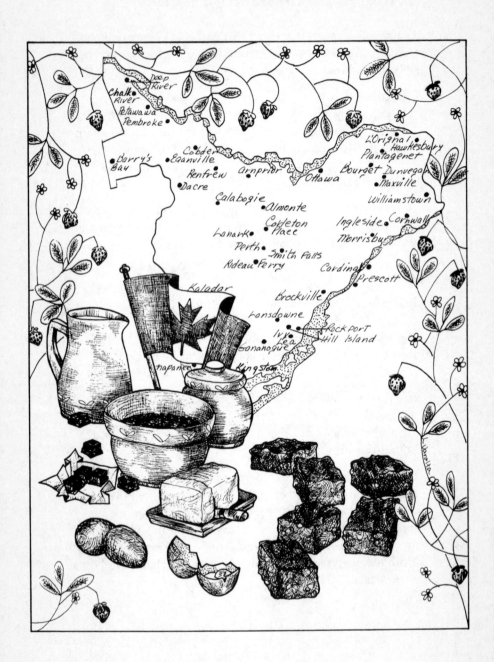

Deep River
Chalk River
Petawawa
Pembroke

Barry's Bay
Cobden
Eganville
Renfrew
Dacre
Arnprior
Ottawa

L'Orignal
Hawkesbury
Plantagenet
Bourget Dunvegan
Maxville
Williamstown

Calabogie
Almonte
Carleton Place
Lanark
Perth
Rideau Ferry
Smith Falls
Ingleside Cornwall
Morrisburg
Cardinal
Prescott

Kaladar
Brockville
Lansdowne
Ivy Lea
Gananoque
Napanee
Kingston
Rock Port
Hill Island

CHAPTER 6

CAPITAL CUISINE

*There is a wealth of tradition in the
historic architecture and the green
pastures of the Ottawa Valley. Politics are not the
only game in town, though, and there are fine dining
rooms in abundance. Rivers separate the region from
Quebec to the east and the United States to the south, but
the culinary life of this historic place is a rich mix of
Québécoise, English, Middle Eastern, European, and the
cultural mosaic that makes up the region around
the nation's capital.*

Recipes

Restaurants of the Region

ALMONTE

Waterford Tea Room • A charming spot for homemade bread, baking, and light lunches

BARRY'S BAY

Siberia Inn • Steak and mashed potatoes are special

DEEP RIVER

Madolyn's Tea Room • Small menu, fresh, well-prepared dishes

GANANOQUE

The Athlone Inn • International cuisine and schnitzels

KINGSTON

Chez Piggy • An experience. A large, eclectic, funky menu

Golden Rooster • Delicatessen

Mino's Place • A Greek dining counter up front with a formal back dining room

Reuben's Deli • Montreal smoked meat and bagels

The Summer Pantry • The outdoor courtyard behind city hall boasts umbrella tables and exactly the kind of light delicious summer food you want

MANOTICK

The Miller's Oven • A voluntary operation in an old house. The seniors cook and the high-schoolers serve. Honest and simple cooking

OTTAWA

The Black Cat • Indoors or outdoors for delicious small meals

Café Marie Antoinette • A tiny Old World tea and pastry shop

Danwhich of Copenhagen • Smorgasbord sandwiches

Il Vagabondo • Excellent northern Italian dining

La Grenouille Et . . . • Fine French cuisine

Le Jardin • A very pretty, tiny two-storey house with patio dining and a fine kitchen

Mama Theresa's • A wonderful, large Italian dining room with a huge menu

Mandarin Court • Large portions from a variety of oriental cuisines

The Mill Dining Lounge • A huge stone mill, serving standard steaks and chops

Sitar • A northern Indian restaurant with a tandoori oven

PALMER RAPIDS

Wingle Inn • For plain, good cooking hidden in bush country

PEMBROKE

Treadles • An unusual, imaginative menu in a charming café

PERTH

Maximillian • Traditional, generous German cooking

SMITHS FALLS

The Bohemia • A stylish, quiet, Czech dining room

Quick Thousand Islands Dressing

At the turn of the century, George Boldt, owner of New York's posh Waldorf Astoria Hotel, erected a tribute of love for his wife, Louise – a castle on Heart Island, one of the Thousand Islands. It was to be the Boldt family summer home. Oscar, their personal chef, was so taken by the beauty of the surroundings that he created a unique salad dressing in honour of the region. The castle was never completed, but the salad dressing lives on.

1 cup mayonnaise
2 tbsp. chili sauce
1 tbsp. sweet pickle
　relish

1 tbsp. minced green
　pepper

Combine all ingredients. Mix well. Serve over chilled lettuce or green salad.

Makes about 1 cup.

Low-Calorie Thousand Islands Dressing

½ cup plain yogurt
½ cup chili sauce
2 tbsp. lemon juice
2 tbsp. sweet pickle
　relish
1 tsp. salt
2 tsp. minced onion

1 tbsp. chopped green
　pepper
1 tsp. Worcestershire
　sauce
1 hard-cooked egg,
　chopped

Combine all ingredients and mix well. Good with green salad. This dressing keeps for several days in the refrigerator.

Makes about 1 cup.

Icelandic Brown Bread

The great gun in Majors Hill Park is fired every day at noon. It's lunch time. There are many restaurants in Ottawa, or take a stroll through the Byward Market where, since 1830, farmers have brought their produce to sell to city folk. A hard-boiled egg or a fresh tomato needs only a dash of salt and a loaf of bread to make them complete. Pick your lunch from the various stalls and eat it alfresco along the banks of the Rideau Canal.

2 cups milk	2 packages yeast
¼ cup shortening	2 cups all-purpose flour
¼ cup brown sugar	2 cups dark rye flour
½ cup molasses	2 cups whole-wheat
1 tbsp. salt	flour
2 tsp. sugar	2 cups bran
¾ cup warm water	

In the top of a double boiler over hot water, scald the milk. Add shortening, brown sugar, molasses, and salt and cool to lukewarm.

In a small bowl, dissolve sugar in warm water. Add yeast and let stand for 10 minutes.

Pour lukewarm milk into a large bowl; stir in the yeast. Stir in the all-purpose flour, then gradually add the rest of the flours and the bran. Turn dough out onto a lightly floured board and knead well, or until dough is easy to handle. Place in a buttered bowl, turning once to grease top. Cover and let rise in a warm place for about 1 hour and 30 minutes, or until double in bulk. Punch dough down and form into 2 loaves. Place loaves in two buttered 8 by 4-inch pans; cover and let rise for about 1 hour, or until loaves have doubled in bulk.

Brush tops of loaves with cold water, then set in a 400°F oven. Immediately turn heat down to 325°F. Bake for 45 minutes, or until loaves sound hollow when tapped.

Makes 2 loaves.

Note: This bread is also good if you use 2 cups of graham flour instead of the rye flour.

Carbonade of Beef Flamande

The meat-and-potatoes person will enjoy this tasty stew.

3 lbs. boneless chuck
½ cup butter
5 large onions, chopped
3 tbsp. all-purpose
    flour
1 tsp. sugar
1 cup brown beef
    stock
1 pint dark beer
1 tbsp. vinegar

1 tsp. finely chopped
    garlic
1 tsp. thyme
Salt
Freshly ground pepper
4 sprigs parsley
2 celery tops
1 bay leaf
2 tbsp. finely chopped
    parsley

Cut the beef into 2-inch pieces. In a Dutch oven or large saucepan, heat half the butter. Add the meat and cook over medium-high heat until meat is well-browned on both sides. Remove meat and set aside.

Add the onions to the saucepan with remaining butter and cook until light brown. Stir in flour and sugar and cook until onions are well browned. Stir in beef stock and beer. Bring liquid to a boil, then stir in vinegar, garlic, and thyme.

Return meat to the pan. Add salt and pepper. With kitchen string, tie together the parsley, celery tops, and bay leaf; add to saucepan. Cover tightly and simmer for 3 hours, or until the meat is tender. To serve, sprinkle with chopped parsley.

Sausage in Brioche

The influence of Québécois cuisine is evident in and near Ottawa.

Brioche

1½ cups all-purpose flour
1½ tsp. yeast
 ¼ cup warm water
 ½ tbsp. sugar

½ tsp. salt
2 large eggs
6 tbsp. unsalted butter,
 softened

Sausage

1 1¼ lb. sausage
 2 cups chicken stock
 1 cup dry white wine

2 tbsp. minced white
 scallions

Glaze

 1 egg yolk

1 tsp. water

Mustard sauce

 1 tbsp. Dijon mustard
 1 tbsp. butter, at room
  temperature
1½ tsp. cornstarch

1 cup sausage-
 poaching liquid
⅓ cup whipping (35%)
 cream

To make brioche: Measure flour into a bowl. In a separate bowl, dissolve yeast in warm water; add 2 tbsp. flour from the bowl and whisk until smooth. Cover and let stand in a warm place for 15 to 20 minutes, or until mixture has doubled in volume. Stir sugar and salt into remaining flour in the bowl.

In a large bowl, beat eggs well. Pour yeast mixture into eggs, then add softened butter. Add flour mixture in four batches, mixing after each addition. Turn dough out onto a floured surface and knead for about 10 minutes, or until dough is smooth and sticky.

Transfer dough to a greased bowl. Cover and let stand in a warm place about 1 hour and 30 minutes, or until dough has tripled in size.

To prepare the sausage: In a 2-quart ovenproof pan, cover the sausage with stock, wine, and minced scallions. Cover and bake on the middle rack of a 375°F oven for 30 minutes. Remove the sausage and let cool, making sure it is straight and the ends do not curve. Reserve 1 cup of pan liquid for sauce. When sausage is cool enough to handle, remove the sausage casing. Allow sausage meat to cool to room temperature, then roll in flour to coat well.

When brioche dough has risen, remove from the bowl and place on a floured surface. The dough should be soft but firm enough to handle. Sprinkle flour all over the dough and flour a rolling pin. Gently, without pressure, roll the dough to a 10 by 10-inch square. Wrap the sausage in the dough. Place the bundle, seam-side down, in a buttered 9 by 5-inch loaf pan. Let brioche rise for about 1 hour, or until it fills most of the pan.

To make glaze: In a small bowl, mix egg yolk and water. Brush glaze over the brioche. Bake brioche on the middle rack of a 400°F oven for 30 minutes, or until brioche is golden brown. Let the loaf cool in the loaf pan for a few minutes, then remove it from the pan and let it cool on a rack for 30 minutes more.

While loaf is cooling, prepare mustard sauce. In a bowl, blend the mustard, butter, and cornstarch until mixture is smooth. Skim any grease off the reserved 1 cup of sausage-poaching liquid and pour liquid into a small saucepan. Add cream and bring to a boil. Whisk the mustard mixture into the boiling liquid. Cook over high heat, stirring constantly, until the sauce thickens slightly. Remove from heat and let cool slightly.

When brioche loaf is cool, slice and serve with warm mustard sauce.

Serves 8.

Tourtière Turnovers

Ottawa and Hull, Quebec, are connected not only geographically but also by their food preferences – particularly for Québécois specialties.

1 *cup butter, softened*	¼ *tsp. dry mustard*
1 *cup (8 oz.) cream*	⅛ *tsp. dried thyme*
cheese, softened	½ *cup hot water*
2½ *cups all-purpose flour*	*Salt*
1 *tsp. salt*	*Pepper*
1 *lb. ground pork*	1 *medium potato,*
1 *onion, minced*	*boiled and mashed*
1 *bay leaf*	1 *egg*
¼ *tsp. dried savory*	1 *tsp. water*
¼ *tsp. ground cloves*	

In a large mixing bowl, cream together butter and cream cheese. Sift together flour and salt, and stir into butter a half-cup at a time. Beat well. Form dough into a ball, dust with flour, and flatten slightly. Wrap dough in waxed paper and chill for at least 3 hours.

In a large skillet, combine pork, onion, bay leaf, savory, cloves, mustard, thyme, hot water, salt, and pepper. Bring to a boil. Simmer, stirring, for 20 minutes. Remove bay leaf. Pour meat mixture into a large bowl and let it cool, then add mashed potato and mix well.

On a lightly floured board, cut the chilled dough in half. Roll each half out until dough is about one-eighth inch thick, then cut into 4-inch rounds. In a small bowl, beat together egg and water. Brush rounds of dough with egg wash, then place 1 tbsp. of meat-potato filling in the centre of each round. Fold in half, pressing and sealing edges with a fork. Brush tops with egg wash. Place rounds on a greased and floured cookie sheet.

Bake in a 350°F oven for 15 to 20 minutes, or until turnovers are brown.

Makes 3 dozen turnovers.

Tomato Butter

Try this at your own risk. You'll never eat a conventional ketchup again. In the Ottawa Valley, three generations have been making this tomato butter.

10 *lbs. ripe tomatoes*	1 *tbsp. mixed pickling*
2 *cups white vinegar*	*spice*
3 *cups finely chopped*	3 *cups apple-cider*
celery	*vinegar*
2 *or 3 apples, sliced*	2 *sticks cinnamon*
or chopped	3 *lbs. sugar*
1 *tbsp. coarse salt*	1 *tsp. cayenne pepper*

Blanch tomatoes; peel them, then chop or slice them and place them in a big pot. Pour white vinegar over tomatoes and allow to stand overnight.

Add celery and apples and boil till thick, stirring occasionally. Place coarse salt and pickling spice in a cheesecloth bag. Add apple-cider vinegar, spice bag, and cinnamon sticks to tomatoes. Add sugar and cayenne pepper. Boil again for 10 to 15 minutes, or until mixture is thick. Remove spice bag and cinnamon sticks. Adjust seasoning. Pour into sterilized jars and seal.

Makes eight 6-oz. jars.

German Cabbage Squares (Kraut Barracks)

So you think hamburgers and buns are all the same? This recipe will change your mind.

Dough

2 tsp. sugar
½ cup lukewarm water
1 package yeast
1 cup milk
¼ cup margarine

6 to 7 cups all-
   purpose flour
1 tsp. salt
¼ cup cold water
2 eggs, beaten

Filling

1 lb. hamburger
1 medium onion,
   minced
Salt

Pepper
Pinch ground allspice
1 cup finely chopped
   cabbage

In a small bowl, dissolve sugar in lukewarm water. Add yeast and let stand for about 10 minutes. Meanwhile, in a saucepan, place milk and margarine. Heat to scalding, then let cool. In a large bowl, stir together flour and salt. Add cooled milk, yeast, cold water, and eggs. Mix until dough is well combined and can be formed into a ball. Place dough in a greased bowl, turning once to grease the top. Cover and let rise in a warm place until double in bulk, about 1 hour and 30 minutes.

While dough is rising, prepare filling. In a skillet, stir together hamburger, onion, salt, pepper, and allspice. Cook over medium heat just until onion is soft and meat is no longer pink. Lift meat out with a slotted spoon and place in a bowl; set aside. To the same skillet, add cabbage and stir. Cook just until soft. Lift cabbage out with a slotted spoon and add to hamburger. Mix hamburger and cabbage and allow to cool.

When dough has risen, punch down and turn out onto a lightly floured board. Roll dough out and cut into 20 squares. Place 1 tbsp. meat-and-cabbage mixture in the middle of each square and seal. Place squares sealed-side down on a greased cookie sheet. Let squares rise, uncovered, for about 1 hour, then bake in a 350°F oven for 20 to 25 minutes, or until squares are golden brown.

Makes 20 squares.

Mrs. Stitt's Beet Salad

An old Canadian recipe to put a little colour in winter meals.

3 quarts small beets	**2 tsp. mustard**
2 cups vinegar	**1 tsp. salt**
2 cups sugar	**½ cup all-purpose flour**
1 cup water	

Place beets in boiling water and cook until tender. Remove from heat and drain. When beets are cool, remove skins and dice beets.

In a saucepan, combine vinegar, sugar, water, mustard, salt, and flour. Mix well. Bring to a boil and cook, stirring occasionally, until mixture thickens. Pour over diced cooked beets and mix well. Pack into sterilized jars and seal. Keeps all winter.

Makes 3 quarts.

Double-Fudge Nut Brownies

Drive to Smiths Falls for dessert. The Hershey Chocolate Company provides guided tours of its operation, as well as delicious samples fresh from the bubbling vats of chocolate.

½ cup butter
½ cup sugar
¼ cup brown sugar
2 tsp. vanilla
⅓ cup honey
2 eggs

½ cup all-purpose flour
⅓ cup cocoa
½ tsp. salt
⅔ cup chopped pecans
½ cup chocolate chips

In the large bowl of an electric mixer, on medium speed, cream butter, sugar, brown sugar, and vanilla. Blend in honey. Add eggs and beat well.

In a separate bowl, combine flour, cocoa, and salt; gradually add flour mixture to creamed mixture. Stir in pecans and chocolate chips. Pour batter into greased 9 by 9-inch pan. Bake in a 350°F oven for 40 minutes, or until brownies begin to pull away from the edge of the pan.

When brownies are cool, cut into 1½-inch squares. These brownies are good with vanilla ice cream.

Makes 36 brownies.

Ginger Balls

In the Ottawa Valley, you can take a farm vacation, stay at a bed-and-breakfast, and eat the kind of hearty Canadian home cooking you don't find in city cafés.

⅓ cup melted
   shortening
⅓ cup sugar
1 cup light molasses
1 egg, beaten
3 cups all-purpose flour

1 tsp. baking soda
1 tsp. cinnamon
½ tsp. cloves
½ tsp. ginger
½ tsp. salt
Sugar

In a large bowl, cream shortening and sugar. Stir in molasses and egg. In a separate bowl, combine flour, baking soda, cinnamon, cloves, ginger, and salt. Add flour mixture gradually to molasses mixture. Stir until dough is smooth.

Mould into 1-inch balls, roll balls in sugar, and bake in a 375°F oven for 10 to 15 minutes, or until ginger balls are light brown.

Makes about 4 dozen.

Nutmeg Feather Cake

A sophisticated cake for adults.

¼ cup butter or margarine	2 tsp. nutmeg
¼ cup shortening	1 tsp. baking soda
1½ cups sugar	1 tsp. baking powder
½ tsp. vanilla	¼ tsp. salt
4 eggs, beaten	1 cup buttermilk
2 cups sifted all-purpose flour	Icing sugar

In a large bowl, cream butter and shortening. Gradually add sugar and beat until light. Beat in vanilla. Add eggs and beat until light and fluffy.

Sift together flour, nutmeg, soda, baking powder, and salt. Alternately add flour and buttermilk to creamed mixture, beating well after each addition. Pour batter into a greased 12 by 9 by 2-inch pan. Bake in a 350°F oven for 35 to 40 minutes, or until toothpick inserted in centre of cake comes out clean. When cake is cool, sprinkle with icing sugar.

Makes 1 cake.

Vineterta (Icelandic Torte)

An unusual confection. Once you've tried this exotic cake, it could become your favourite "show-off" dish.

Batter

¾ cup butter or
   margarine
2 cups sugar
4 eggs
1 tsp. ground
   cardamom

½ tsp. vanilla
1 tbsp. water
5 cups all-purpose flour
3 tsp. baking powder

Filling

1½ lbs. prunes
1 cup sugar
¼ tsp. salt

½ tsp. vanilla
½ tsp. cinnamon

Icing

¼ cup butter
2 cups sifted icing
   sugar

1½ tbsp. milk or cereal
   (10%) cream
1 tsp. almond extract

To make the batter: In a large bowl, cream the butter and sugar. Add eggs one at a time, beating after each addition. Add cardamom, vanilla, and water. Sift together flour and baking powder and add to creamed mixture. On a floured surface, roll out the dough. Cut it in half, then cut each half into 6 portions. Roll each portion into a 9-inch circle. Place a circle on the bottom of an inverted 9-inch round cake pan. Bake the circles in a 375°F oven for 10 to 15 minutes, or until golden. Repeat until all layers are baked.

While layers are baking, make the filling. In a saucepan, cover prunes with water. Bring to a boil and cook until soft. Drain. When prunes are cool, remove pits; then mash the prunes, or purée them in the blender. Return purée to saucepan and add sugar, salt, vanilla, and cinnamon. Bring to a boil and cook for 5 minutes, stirring constantly. Remove from heat and let cool.

Spread an equal amount of filling on each of 5 layers, then stack 6 layers to make a cake, using one of the unfilled layers as the top layer. Repeat with other 6 layers.

To make icing: In a bowl, cream the butter. Gradually stir in the icing sugar alternately with the milk; beat well. Stir in almond extract. Spread icing on top of cake. Allow it to drip down the sides if it wants to.

Place cakes in cookie tins or cover with waxed paper. Let set for 3 to 4 days before cutting.

Makes 2 cakes.

Creamy Rhubarb Pie

There's a reason rhubarb was always called "pie plant": it lends itself perfectly to that medium.

Pastry for double-crust
9-inch pie
(see page 95)
3 cups finely chopped
rhubarb (about
10 medium stalks)

1 tbsp. butter
1 cup sugar
2 eggs
¼ tsp. nutmeg
2 tbsp. all-purpose
flour

Line a 9-inch pie plate with pastry. Place rhubarb in bottom crust.

In a large bowl, cream butter and sugar. Add eggs and beat until mixture is light and fluffy. Add nutmeg and flour and beat until creamy. Pour mixture over rhubarb and cover with top crust. Bake in a 450°F oven for 10 minutes, then turn oven down to 350°F and bake for 30 to 35 minutes more, until crust is golden brown.

Makes one 9-inch pie.

Apple-Cheese-Nut Pie

Pastry for a double-crust
    9-inch pie
    (see page 95)
4 cups thinly sliced
    apples
¾ cup brown sugar
1 tbsp. all-purpose
    flour

½ tsp. cinnamon
¾ tsp. nutmeg
¼ cup broken walnut
    meats
¼ lb. sharp Cheddar
    cheese, cut into
    ½-inch cubes

Line a 9-inch pie pan with pastry and arrange half the apple slices on the bottom crust.

In a small bowl, combine sugar, flour, cinnamon, and nutmeg. Sprinkle half the mixture over the apples in pie. Sprinkle half the walnuts over pie; add half the cheese cubes. Then add a second layer of apples, the rest of the sugar-flour mixture, remaining nuts, and remaining cheese.

Cover pie with top crust, pressing edges together with a fork. Prick the surface with fork. Bake in a 425°F oven for 40 to 45 minutes, or until apples are tender.

Makes one 9-inch pie.

Aunt Jean's Pie

Not mad about pie? You'll change your mind with this one.

Pastry for 1-crust 9-inch
    deep-dish pie
    (see page 95)
2 cups strawberries,
    hulled

2 cups diced rhubarb
2 cups sour cream
1 egg
1½ cups sugar
⅓ cup all-purpose flour

Topping

½ cup all-purpose flour
½ cup brown sugar

¼ cup butter

Line a 9-inch deep-dish pie plate with pastry. Stir together strawberries and diced rhubarb; pour into pie plate.

In a separate bowl, stir together sour cream, egg, sugar, and flour. Pour over strawberries and rhubarb.

To make topping: Stir together flour, brown sugar, and butter. Sprinkle topping over pie. Bake in a 450°F oven for 15 minutes; then turn oven down to 350°F and bake for 30 minutes more, or until crust and topping are golden brown.

Makes one 9-inch deep pie.

Note: Filling and topping can also be used to make two 9-inch pies. Divide your pastry in half and line 2 regular pie plates; divide filling and topping evenly between the two.

Belgian Honey Cake (Zoetekock)

Thanks to Granny Verhaeghe for carrying this recipe across the Atlantic from Belgium.

3 cups sifted all-purpose flour
¾ cup liquid honey
3 tsp. baking powder
½ cup evaporated milk
½ cup water
1 cup brown sugar
¼ tsp. anise extract or 1 tsp. anisette liqueur
1 egg
1 tsp. molasses

Combine all ingredients and mix well. Pour batter in an 8 by 4-inch loaf pan and bake in a 350°F oven for 45 minutes to 1 hour, or until a toothpick inserted in the centre comes out clean.

Makes 1 cake.

Mrs. Webber's Spiced Crab Apples

If you're lucky enough to beat the birds to the apple trees, you'll have a delicious, spicy condiment all winter.

2½ lbs. crab apples
Cloves
1½ cups water

1½ cups vinegar
4 cups sugar
1 oz. stick cinnamon

Stick 1 whole clove into each apple. In a large pot, combine water, vinegar, sugar, and cinnamon. Heat, stirring, until sugar dissolves. Bring to a boil. Drop in apples and cook just until tender; apples should remain whole. Remove cinnamon stick. Place whole apples in sterilized jars and add syrup to cover, leaving one-quarter-inch head space. Seal. Cool and label.

Serve with hot or cold meat – ham, pork, sausages.

Makes 8 cups.

Blueberry and Raspberry Pie

These mixed berries capture the flavour of summer.

Pastry for 1-crust 9-inch
  pie (see page 95)
2 cups blueberries
1¼ cups raspberries

1 cup water
¾ cup sugar
1½ tbsp. cornstarch

Line a 9-inch pie plate with pastry. Pour blueberries into pie. Add ¼ cup of the raspberries.

In a saucepan, cook remaining 1 cup raspberries in water for 5 minutes. In a small bowl, combine sugar and cornstarch. Add to saucepan and cook, stirring constantly, for about 4 or 5 minutes, or until glaze thickens. Pour glaze over pie. Refrigerate for 3 or 4 hours; serve cold.

Makes one 9-inch pie.

Aunt Edna's Strawberry Bread

A lovely tea-time dainty.

3 *eggs*	1 *tbsp. cinnamon*
2 *cups sugar*	1 *tsp. baking soda*
1 *cup salad oil*	1 *tsp. salt*
1 *tsp. vanilla*	½ *tsp. baking powder*
2 *cups all-purpose flour*	2 *cups fresh*
1 *cup rolled oats*	*strawberries*

In a large bowl, cream together eggs and sugar. Beat in oil and vanilla.

In a separate bowl, combine flour, oats, cinnamon, baking soda, salt, and baking powder. Beat into egg-sugar mixture. Crush strawberries, then add to batter and mix well. Pour batter into two greased and floured 8 by 4-inch loaf pans. Bake in a 350°F oven for 1 hour, or until toothpick inserted in the centre comes out clean.

Makes 2 loaves.

Note: You can also use frozen strawberries or strawberry jam to make this bread. If you use frozen berries, you will need 2 cups of drained berries. Or use 1 cup of jam, and use only 1½ cups sugar.

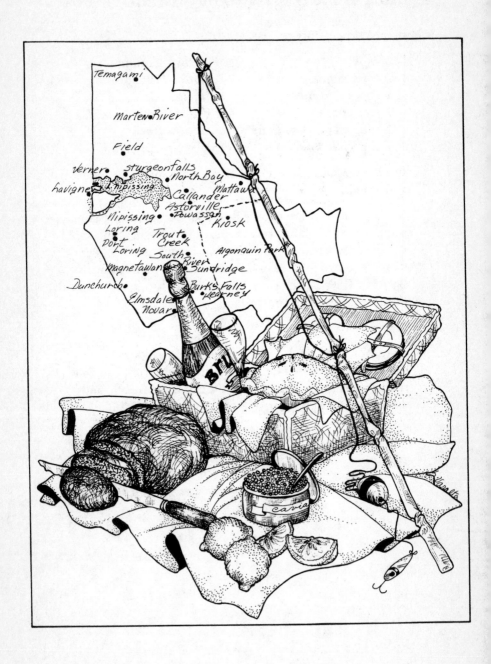

162

CHAPTER 7

NORTHWEST TERRITORY

The land of Indian legend, the route of the voyageurs, and a dream come true for sport fishermen. Cold northern lakes team with bass, pike, muskellunge, and more. In Algonquin Park, the unspoiled wilderness is criss-crossed with canoe routes and hiking trails. The tall pines shelter wild flowers, herbs, and game in this rocky terrain.

Recipes

Restaurants of the Region

ALGONQUIN PARK

Arowhon Pines • The dining room ranks as one of the best in rural Ontario. One of summer's most delicious memories is dinner on the weathered log terrace at the Pines overlooking the tranquillity of Joe Lake, and watching the sun set

Killarney Lodge • A fifty-year-old lodge of log construction, naturally landscaped with multi-coloured flowers. The interior exudes a warmth that comes from decades of loving care

NORTH BAY

The Lions Heart • A popular British-style pub with well-prepared food

Matilda's Roman Villa • Homemade pasta and great sandwiches for the road

Old Chicago • Chinese cuisine in modern surroundings

Traditions • An elegant continental dining room in one of the town's early homes

PARRY SOUND

Rocky Crest Resort • New resort on the shores of Lake Joseph with a dining lounge that offers continental cuisine

TEMAGAMI

Angus Lake Lodge • Schnitzels, strudels, and home baking

TROUT CREEK

Glen Roberts Tea Room • You'll feel you've stumbled into a story book. Everything is made on the premises by Tom and Peggy Ludlow. The food is superb

Russian Black Bread

A far cry from white sliced sandwich loaf. This is the real thing.

2½ cups cold water	4 cups rye flour
¼ cup butter	2 cups 100% bran
¼ cup vinegar	cereal (e.g.,
¼ cup dark molasses	All-Bran)
1 oz. unsweetened	2 tbsp. caraway seeds,
baking chocolate,	crushed
coarsely chopped	2 tsp. instant-coffee
1 tsp. sugar	granules
½ cup warm water	1 tsp. salt
2 packages yeast	4 to 5 cups unbleached
	all-purpose flour

Glaze

¼ tsp. cornstarch	¼ cup warm water

In a large saucepan over medium heat, stir together cold water, butter, vinegar, molasses, and chocolate. Heat, stirring frequently, until chocolate is melted and ingredients are thoroughly blended. Remove from heat; let cool to lukewarm. Meanwhile, in a large bowl, dissolve sugar in warm water and sprinkle in yeast. Let stand until yeast is dissolved, about 5 minutes. Add lukewarm chocolate mixture to yeast and stir until thoroughly blended.

In a second large bowl, stir together rye flour, bran cereal, caraway seeds, coffee granules, salt, and 3 cups of the white flour. Stir flour mixture, 1 cup at a time, into yeast mixture; mix until dough begins to leave the sides of the bowl. Add as much of the remaining white flour as you need to make a stiff dough. Turn dough out onto a lightly floured surface. Knead, incorporating more flour as necessary, until dough is smooth and elastic. This will take 10 to 15 minutes. Shape dough into a ball and place in a large buttered bowl, turning to coat evenly with butter. Let rise, covered with a kitchen towel, in a warm, draft-free place until doubled in bulk, about 1 hour and 30 minutes.

Punch dough down and turn out onto a floured board. Cover with the greased bowl and let rest for about 5 minutes. While dough is resting, lightly butter two 8-inch round cake pans. Divide dough into 2 equal balls. Flatten each ball with the heel of your hand to form circles, then reshape it into a ball by pulling the edges in and tucking them under. Place each ball of dough, seam-side down, in a lightly greased, 8-inch round cake pan. Cover pans with a kitchen towel; let loaves rise in a warm, draft-free place until doubled in bulk, about 1 hour. Bake in a 350°F oven for about 45 minutes, or until loaves sound hollow when tapped lightly with your knuckles.

While the bread is baking, make the glaze. In a small saucepan over high heat, stir together cornstarch and warm water. Boil for 1 minute, then remove from heat. When bread is done, remove from oven and brush cornstarch mixture lightly over tops of loaves. Return loaves to oven and bake for 5 minutes more. Turn onto wire racks. Cool completely before slicing.

Makes two 8-inch round loaves.

Pumpkin Soup

There are always extra pumpkins around on October 31. A delicious use for this florid fall produce.

1 ½ cups packed fresh
  breadcrumbs
2 6 to 7 lb. pumpkins
⅔ cup minced onion
6 tbsp. butter
½ tsp. salt
Pepper
Pinch nutmeg
½ tsp. ground sage

½ cup finely diced or
  coarsely grated
  Swiss cheese
Chicken stock
  (about 10 cups)
1 bay leaf
½ cup whipping (35%)
  cream
Fresh parsley

In a large shallow pan or on a cookie sheet, spread breadcrumbs. Set in a 300°F oven to dry for about 15 minutes, stirring occasionally. Meanwhile, cut lids from pumpkins, being careful not to break off the stems. Clean out both pumpkins thoroughly.

In a skillet, sauté onion in butter until onion is tender and translucent. Stir in breadcrumbs and let cook slowly for about 2 minutes, so that breadcrumbs absorb butter. Stir in salt, pepper, nutmeg, and sage. Remove from heat and stir in cheese, then spoon mixture into one of the pumpkins. Pour in chicken stock to within a half-inch of top of pumpkin. Float bay leaf on top of stock; replace lid. Set pumpkin on a cookie sheet.

Bake pumpkin in a 400°F oven for 1 hour and 30 minutes. The pumpkin should start to soften on the outside, and the chicken stock should be bubbling. Reduce heat to 350°F and bake for another 30 minutes. The pumpkin will be tender but should still hold its shape.

Remove pumpkin from oven, lift lid, and carefully ladle the soup into a heavy saucepan. On a tray, split baked pumpkin in half. Scrape out the insides and add to soup; discard skin.

Slowly bring soup and pumpkin pulp to a boil, stirring occasionally. Remove from heat and stir in cream. Chop fresh parsley and stir in. Carefully transfer soup to second pumpkin shell and serve.

Serves 12.

Arowhon Pines Goulash Soup

A hearty meal – good after a day outdoors.

2 tbsp. butter	2 cups beef stock
2 tbsp. vegetable oil	1 can tomato paste
½ tsp. thyme	¼ tsp. caraway seeds
1 tsp. paprika	2 bay leaves
1½ lbs. beef, diced	1 clove fresh garlic
2 onions, sliced	Salt
2 carrots, diced	Pepper
2 celery stalks, diced	

In a large frying pan, melt butter and oil. Stir in thyme and paprika. Add beef cubes and brown. With a slotted spoon, remove beef cubes. To the same saucepan, add onion; sauté slowly until onions are golden. Add carrots and celery and sauté briefly – carrots and celery should remain crunchy.

In a large saucepan, bring beef stock to a boil. Add tomato paste. Add caraway seeds, bay leaves, and garlic. Add sautéed vegetables and diced beef. Simmer until beef and vegetables are tender. Salt and pepper to taste.

This soup is good served with dill pickles and fresh bread and butter.

Serves 6.

Herb Vinegar

In days gone by, to ensure a proper balance of acidity, the town's vinegar-maker would whisper the name of the county's most acid-tongued, sour-faced women into the bung-hole of the wooden vinegar cask. Excellent balance was guaranteed.

> **Large bunch fresh**
> **tarragon, thyme,**
> **mint, or oregano**
> **3 cups wine vinegar**

Wash herbs and pat dry. Discard stalks. Bruise leaves gently with your fingers and pack into a glass jar or stone crock. Cover with vinegar and leave for 4 to 6 weeks. Strain and pour liquid into bottles. Place a sprig of fresh herb in the bottle to add flavour and to identify the contents.

Makes 3 cups.

Nasturtium Vinegar

> **Several handfuls of**
> **nasturtiums**
> **½ tsp. cayenne pepper**
> **Pinch salt**
> **3 cups wine vinegar**

Pick your nasturtiums on a dry day. You should have about 2 cups. Place the flowers in a crock or a glass jar and add cayenne pepper and salt. Pour in vinegar. Cover and let steep for 10 days, then strain and pour into glass bottles.

Makes 3 cups.

Apricot Chutney

Driving the country roads around Nipissing, Corbeil, Callander, Trout Creek, and Powassan, there is an enclave of arts-and-crafts people, antique shops, museums, and tea rooms operated by people who believe in a renewed appreciation of the simpler life. Herb gardens abound and add piquancy to these artists' tables.

This chutney complements every dish, from ice cream to roast meats. You'll wish you'd made more.

2 lbs. dried apricots
3 cups brown sugar
2 tsp. whole coriander
2 onions, thinly sliced
5 cloves garlic, minced

2 tbsp. coarse salt
2 tbsp. grated fresh ginger
1 cup sultana raisins
2 cups cider vinegar

Soak the apricots in cold water for 8 hours. Drain well, then place in a heavy saucepan. Stir in brown sugar, coriander, onion slices, garlic, salt, ginger, raisins, and vinegar. Cook, uncovered, over low heat for 40 minutes to 1 hour, stirring often. The chutney should have the consistency of jam. Pour into sterilized jars and seal.

Makes 6 cups.

Brandied Blackberry Pie

A fitting tribute to this lush berry.

Pastry for a 2-crust
9-inch pie (see
page 95)
5 cups ripe blackberries
Fresh lemon juice
1 cup sugar

⅓ cup apple brandy
1¼ cups breadcrumbs
4 tbsp. butter, melted

Line a 9-inch pie pan with pastry; refrigerate. Place the blackberries in a large bowl. Squeeze lemon juice over berries; sprinkle with sugar and brandy. Set aside. In a small bowl, drizzle breadcrumbs with melted butter; toss to coat. Let stand for about 5 minutes.

Remove pastry-lined pie pan from refrigerator. Stir buttered breadcrumbs into blackberries; spoon berries evenly into pie crust. Moisten edge of crust with water. Fold pastry top into quarters; carefully place over filling in pie. Unfold pastry and centre over filling. Fold edges under rim of pie plate; pinch with thumb and index finger to make a decorative edge. Make four 1-inch slashes in top crust.

Place pie pan on a baking sheet and set on the centre rack of the oven. Bake in a 375°F oven for 45 to 50 minutes, or until top crust is golden brown.

Makes one 9-inch pie.

Note: For a shinier crust, brush top crust lightly with 1 egg yolk beaten with 1 tbsp. milk just before baking. This pie is also good made with other flavours of fruit brandy.

Biscuit-Topped Fresh-Fruit Pudding

Berries grow in abundance here, and reach their apex in luscious pies, jams, and puddings.

4 cups blueberries
½ cup sugar

Topping

2 cups sifted all-purpose flour
3 tsp. baking powder
1 tsp. salt

¼ cup sugar
¼ cup plus 2 tbsp. shortening
1 cup milk

In a buttered 8-cup casserole, stir together blueberries and sugar. In a separate bowl, combine flour, baking powder, and salt. Stir in sugar. Cut in shortening; then add milk and mix until flour is just moistened. Spread biscuit topping over fruit.

Bake in a 350°F oven for 1 hour, or until topping is golden brown.

Serves 6 to 8.

Note: This pudding is also delicious with cherries, apples, or peaches.

Mom's Welsh Spotted Dick (Steamed Pudding)

This pudding was brought from Wales in the early 1930s by a fourteen-year-old Bernardi girl, who was coming to work as a housekeeper in Canada. Today her children enjoy making this traditional dessert.

> 2 cups all-purpose flour
> ½ tsp. salt
> ½ tsp. ground allspice
> 2 tsp. baking powder
> ½ cup sugar
> 1 cup dark raisins
> ½ cup currants
> 1 cup ground suet
> 1 cup milk

In a large mixing bowl, combine flour, salt, allspice, and baking powder. Stir in sugar, raisins, and currants. Add suet and stir. Slowly add milk, beating well. When batter becomes too thick to stir, work remaining milk in with your hands.

Place dough in a buttered 5-cup pudding mould. Cover the top of the mould with a large piece of aluminum foil. Make a pleat in the centre of the foil; then tie foil in place around the rim of the mould with string. Put the mould on a steamer rack or an inverted saucer and set in a large saucepan in approximately 3 inches of water. Cover the saucepan and steam the pudding for 2 hours and 30 minutes. Check the level of the water from time to time, and add more if necessary.

To serve, remove the foil and run a knife gently around the pudding. Turn onto a serving plate and serve warm with maple syrup.

Serves 4 to 6.

Chelsea Buns

There's nothing like the country in the summer, and nothing compares to the scent of fresh baking from rustic country kitchens.

2 tsp. sugar	8 cups all-purpose flour
½ cup warm water	1 tsp. cinnamon
⅛ lb. fresh yeast	2 cups brown sugar
3 eggs	1 cup chopped nuts
¾ cup sugar	1 cup butter, at room
1 cup vegetable oil	temperature
2 tsp. salt	½ cup shortening, at
1¾ cups hot water	room temperature

Dissolve the 2 tsp. sugar in warm water. Add yeast, cover, and set in a warm place until mixture begins to bubble, about 10 to 12 minutes.

In a large mixing bowl, beat eggs and the ¾ cup sugar. Add oil and continue to beat. Add salt and hot water, then stir in yeast mixture. Add flour and stir until flour is absorbed. Cover with a towel and set in a warm place. Let rise for 1 hour, or until doubled in bulk.

Divide dough into 3 pieces. On a floured board, roll each piece into a rectangle about one-quarter inch thick. In a small bowl, stir together cinnamon, brown sugar, and chopped nuts. In a separate bowl, mix together butter and shortening. Spread butter mixture over each piece of dough, then sprinkle with cinnamon-sugar mixture. Roll up jelly-roll fashion and pinch edges closed. Cut into slices about 1½ inches thick. Place slices, cut-side down, in well-greased 9-inch round pans; you should fit 6 or 7 slices in each pan. Cover and let rise in a warm place for 1 hour, or until double in bulk. Bake in a 375°F oven for 25 minutes, or until nicely browned.

Makes about 2 dozen buns.

Tom's Buttermilk Scones

Spices and slices make this dessert an unusual adaptation of the original.

1¼ cups all-purpose flour	Few drops of almond
¼ cup plus 1 tbsp.	extract
baking powder	2 cups buttermilk
Pinch salt	⅔ cup brown sugar
¼ cup butter	⅔ cup chopped walnuts
2 eggs	⅔ cup seedless raisins
	Nutmeg or cinnamon

In a large bowl, sift together flour, baking powder, and salt. In a separate bowl, cream the butter. Beat in eggs and almond extract. Pour butter-egg mixture into flour and beat well; beat in buttermilk and brown sugar. Fold in walnuts and raisins.

Pour batter evenly into a greased 9-inch pizza pan and sprinkle with nutmeg or cinnamon. Bake in a 450°F oven for 18 to 20 minutes, or until scone is light brown. Let cool for 10 minutes, then slice as you would a pie. Serve with preserves and ice cream.

Makes 8 slices.

Lake Nipissing Crispy Fish in Batter

Pickerel is called a fisher's steak. Prepared with this crispy batter, it's easy to understand why.

2 cups all-purpose flour	1 tbsp. salad oil
2 tsp. baking powder	1 cup cold water
1¼ tsp. salt	2 lbs. pickerel fillets
2 tsp. sugar	Oil for deep frying
½ tsp. basil	

In a large mixing bowl, combine 1 cup of the flour, baking powder, salt, sugar, and basil. In a separate bowl, combine salad oil and water. Make a well in the flour mixture and slowly pour in oil and water. Blend.

In a saucer, place remaining 1 cup of flour. Dip pickerel fillets in the flour, then coat with batter. Heat oil in deep-fryer to 375°F. Fry fillets for 5 to 7 minutes, or until golden brown.

Serves 6.

Bass Poached in Vegetable Vinaigrette

A picnic in the park means more than you bargained for when you picnic in Algonquin Park, almost three thousand square miles of natural environment criss-crossed with canoe routes, hiking trails, and campgrounds. The wilderness stretches northwest to the legendary land of the Ojibwa and the voyageurs. Bass, trout, pike, pickerel, and muskellunge await you in the clear northern lakes.

3 quarts water
¼ cup cider vinegar
1 carrot, cut into
    matchsticks
2 celery stalks, cut into
    matchsticks
¼ onion, thinly sliced

5 sprigs parsley
1 bay leaf
10 peppercorns
Pinch salt
3 lbs. bass fillets
Fresh lemon

In a large saucepan, bring water and vinegar to a boil. Add carrot, celery, onion, parsley, bay leaf, and peppercorns and bring to a boil again. Add salt and fish fillets and cook for 7 or 8 minutes, or until bass is tender. Serve immediately, garnished with pot vegetables and slices of fresh lemon.

Serves 6.

Note: You can also make this recipe with 1 small whole bass. Fish should be cleaned and gutted. Whole bass should be cooked for 15 to 18 minutes, or until tender.

Buckwheat Crêpes with Caviar

Sturgeon Falls was settled by French-Canadian fishermen about a hundred years ago. Today, the town's fishers bring in the incredible sturgeon. Each fish weighs about a hundred pounds – one pound for every year of its life. Sturgeon have no teeth and no scales, but are filled with a delicacy sought by gourmets the world over – caviar.

The fine quality of Lake Nipissing caviar demands fine presentation. This traditional Russian dish is always appealing.

5 tbsp. unsalted butter	Vegetable oil for frying
1 egg	1 cup cold sour cream
1½ cups milk	2 oz. black caviar
½ tsp. sugar	Lemon wedges
½ tsp. salt	Freshly ground pepper
½ cup buckwheat flour	
½ cup sifted all-purpose flour	

Melt 3 tbsp. of the butter and allow to cool to room temperature. Have egg and milk at room temperature.

In a large mixing bowl, whip the egg until it is light and foamy. Slowly whisk in milk, sugar, salt, and the melted butter. Gradually add buckwheat flour and all-purpose flour, stirring with the whisk until flours are just moistened; do not overmix. Let batter stand, covered, at room temperature, for a few hours or overnight.

Brush skillet with oil. Heat oil. Ladle 2 tbsp. of the batter into the pan; immediately tip the pan and rotate to cover bottom evenly with batter. Pour any excess batter back into bowl. Cook until batter is set, about 1 minute. Turn crêpe. (The easiest way to do this is to use your fingers.) Cook the second side for about 30 seconds. Remove crêpe to ovenproof plate; cover loosely with a kitchen towel. Keep warm in a very low oven. Add a bit of oil to the skillet, if necessary; continue to make crêpes and stack them in the oven until all batter is used.

Melt remaining 2 tbsp. of the butter. Brush each crêpe with melted butter; fold crêpe into quarters. Lift the top layer of each crêpe at the open end and spoon in about 1 tbsp. sour cream. Top cream with about ½ tsp. caviar. Fold back top layer of crêpe so filling is exposed. As each crêpe is filled, arrange on a warmed serving platter. Serve immediately, garnished with lemon wedges and pepper.

Makes 16 crêpes.

Salmon with Lake Nipissing Caviar Sauce

A little caviar goes a long way.

2 8-oz. slices fresh salmon	**2 tbsp. whipping (35%) cream**
Salt	**Juice of 1 lime**
Pepper	**1 egg yolk**
1 tsp. butter	**2 tsp. black Lake Nipissing caviar**
1 tsp. chopped shallots	
2 tbsp. dry white wine	

Season salmon with salt and pepper. In a large skillet, combine butter, shallots, and white wine. Place the salmon in the skillet; place the skillet over high heat. When the wine begins to boil, cover the skillet and lower the heat. Cook for 2 minutes, then turn the heat off. Leave covered skillet on the burner for 8 minutes. Remove salmon from skillet and place it on a serving dish; reserve skillet juices.

In a small heatproof bowl, stir together cream, lime juice, egg yolk, and caviar. Pour in juices from skillet. Stir well; salt and pepper to taste. In a pan of boiling water, place the bowl. Heat the liquid, stirring constantly. When liquid has thickened, pour over the salmon and serve.

Serves 2.

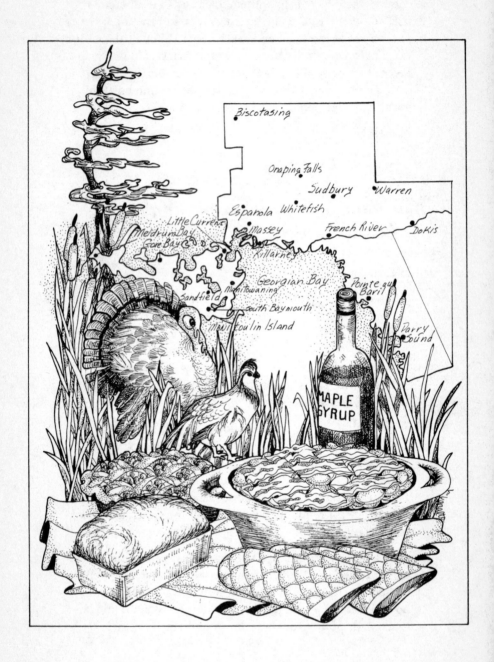

Biscotasing
Onaping Falls
Sudbury   Warren
Espanola Whitefish
Little Current   French River   Dokis
Medrum Bay   Massey
Gore Bay
Killarney
Georgian Bay   Pointe au Baril
Sandfield   Manitowaning
South Baymouth   Parry Sound
Manitoulin Island

MAPLE SYRUP

CHAPTER 8

RAINBOW COUNTRY

Reflections on water have given
this region its name. Springs bubbling
from craggy rocks, rushing white water, and
placid lakes that stretch as far as the eye can see – all are
a joy for anglers and boaters. In the forest, small game
abounds, and for those who forage in nature's vegetable
garden, there's a good crop of greens.

Recipes

Restaurants of the Region

LITTLE CURRENT

Edgewater Restaurant • A view of the water while you dine

MANITOULIN ISLAND, LAKE MINDEMOYA

Rock Garden Terrace • Hearty meals

MELDRUM BAY

Meldrum Bay Inn • Accommodation and meals in a town with a population of fifty

SUDBURY

The Continental • Hotel dining room

Marconi's • A friendly Italian atmosphere

The Peter Piper • A sophisticated hotel with a dining room that offers Italian-style foods

Roast Pheasant

Being married to a film director and actor gives me the opportunity to travel to exotic places. *Adventures in Rainbow Country*, an international television series shot entirely in Whitefish Falls, was the reason for my first visit to northern Ontario. Then, as now, there were very few restaurants in the area, so we did our own cooking. My husband stayed in Whitefish Falls and directed the show, and I, a weekend guest, returned to the city. As a new bride, I felt it was my duty to leave him prepared food, so I spent Sunday over the barbecue – roasting beef on the spit – and in the kitchen – roasting birds in the oven. The moment I left, the ravenous cast and crew descended on my carefully prepared provisions and had a feast. Small wonder I was invited back every weekend.

3 tbsp. butter
1 tsp. sage
2 pheasants
3 tbsp. all-purpose flour
4 slices bacon
1 bunch watercress
1 small onion, finely chopped
½ cup finely sliced mushrooms
1 cup sherry
1 cup beef consommé
Salt
Freshly ground black pepper

In a large roasting pan, melt 2 tbsp. of the butter. Sprinkle sage into pheasant cavities. Divide remaining 1 tbsp. butter and place in cavities. Sprinkle 2 tbsp. of the flour over the pheasants and set them in the roasting pan, breast-side down. Gently brown over medium heat for 2 or 3 minutes. Turn pheasants breast-side up and cover with the bacon slices. Roast in a 400°F oven for 35 minutes, basting with pan juices from time to time. Be careful not to overcook the birds; they should be golden but still juicy.

Place cooked pheasants on a warm serving dish and surround with watercress. Let birds rest for at least 10 minutes before carving.

While birds are resting, skim most of the fat from the roasting pan and discard. You should have about 2 tbsp. of pan juices. Add onion to pan juices and place pan over medium heat. Cook until onion is soft and brown; then add mushrooms, stirring constantly so mushrooms do not burn. Add remaining 1 tbsp. flour; gradually add sherry and beef consommé.

Bring liquid to a boil and simmer for 10 minutes. Skim fat from sauce, season to taste with salt and pepper, and serve in a gravy boat with carved pheasant.

Serves 4.

Rabbit Pie

A dish for the hunter and forager.

8 slices bacon
1 bay leaf
1 lb. mushrooms, sliced
3 leeks, cleaned and
    chopped into
    1-inch pieces
1 2 lb. rabbit, cut into
    small pieces
Salt

Freshly ground black
    pepper
3 tbsp. chopped parsley
3 medium potatoes,
    peeled and cut
    into ¼-inch slices
1 tbsp. wine vinegar

Blanch the bacon in boiling water for 2 minutes. In the bottom of a large, heavy, ovenproof dish, place the bay leaf, covered by 4 slices of the bacon. Cover with half the mushrooms and half the leeks. Add the rabbit pieces and cover with the remaining mushrooms and leeks. Season heavily with salt and pepper. Sprinkle with 2 tbsp. of the parsley. Add the potatoes, making sure that the other vegetables are completely covered. Add a little more salt and pepper; add remaining 1 tbsp. parsley. Cover with remaining 4 bacon slices; pour vinegar over bacon. Cover tightly and bake in a 325°F oven for 2 hours. Do not uncover to look inside!

Serves 6.

Swedish Saffron Bread

A wonderful old-fashioned tea bread, to be served with butter and love.

2 packages yeast	½ cup boiling water
2 tsp. sugar	4 cups all-purpose flour
½ cup warm water	¼ cup light raisins
1 cup milk	¼ cup dried currants
4 tbsp. butter	¼ cup chopped glacé
½ cup sugar	cherries
1 tsp. salt	¼ cup chopped citrus
1 tsp. saffron threads	peel

In a small bowl, stir the 2 tsp. sugar into warm water. Stir in yeast and let stand about 10 minutes. Scald milk. Remove from heat and stir in butter, the ½ cup sugar, and salt. Allow to cool. Meanwhile, in a small bowl, place saffron threads in boiling water. Set aside to cool.

In a large mixing bowl, combine cooled milk and cooled saffron water. Stir in the yeast. Add half the flour and beat well. (You can use an electric mixer for this step.) Add remaining flour and beat in by hand until thoroughly mixed. Stir in the fruit. Turn dough onto a lightly floured board and knead for 8 to 10 minutes, adding flour if dough becomes sticky. (You may use as much as ¼ cup more flour.) Place dough in a greased bowl, turning once to grease the top. Cover and let rise in a warm place until doubled in bulk, about 2 hours.

Punch dough down. Turn out onto a floured board and let rest for 10 minutes. Shape into 2 loaves and place in greased 8½ by 4½ by 2½-inch pans. Let rise until doubled in bulk, about 1 hour and 30 minutes. Bake in a 375°F oven for 45 minutes. Check loaves after 25 minutes. If tops are already brown, cover loaves with foil for the last 20 minutes of baking. Remove loaves from oven and brush tops with butter. Let cool for 10 minutes, then remove loaves from pans and cool on a rack.

Makes 2 loaves.

Whole Baked Whitefish with Cornbread Stuffing

Garnished, the whole fish looks beautiful on the platter; with the stuffing, you'll get a few more servings.

Stuffing

3 cups crumbled Cornbread (see next page)
¼ cup finely chopped onion
2 tbsp. chopped parsley

1½ tsp. crushed thyme
½ tsp. salt
Dash of pepper
1 egg, lightly beaten
¼ cup butter, melted

Fish

1 3 lb. whitefish, scaled, cleaned, and boned
1 tsp. salt

⅛ tsp. pepper
Melted butter
Parsley
Lemon

To prepare stuffing: In a mixing bowl, stir together crumbled cornbread and onion. Stir in parsley, thyme, salt, and pepper. Add egg and melted butter and toss lightly. Set aside.

To prepare fish: Sprinkle interior of fish lightly with salt and pepper. Spoon stuffing into fish. Fasten sides of fish together with wooden toothpicks or small skewers.

Place fish in a large oiled baking dish and brush with melted butter. Bake in a 375°F oven for about 40 minutes, or until fish flakes easily with a fork. Garnish with parsley and fresh lemon wedges.

Serves 4 to 6.

Cornbread

¾ cup all-purpose flour,   1 ¼ cups cornmeal
    sifted   1 egg
3 tsp. baking powder   1 cup milk
½ tsp. salt   3 tbsp. shortening

In a large mixing bowl, sift together flour, baking powder, and salt. Stir in cornmeal. Add egg, milk, and shortening and beat until smooth. (This will take about 1 minute.) Pour batter into an oiled 8-inch square pan. Bake in a 400°F oven for 20 to 25 minutes, or until a toothpick inserted in the centre comes out clean.

Serves 6.

Spruce Grouse en Cocotte

A spruce grouse is a dark-fleshed game bird which feasts on spruce needles in its northern forest habitat.

4 spruce grouse   ½ cup sherry
4 tbsp. all-purpose   1 tsp. salt
    flour   ¼ tsp. black pepper
½ cup butter   2 tbsp. cornstarch
1 cup chicken broth   1 cup sour cream
2 medium onions, sliced
1 10-oz. can whole
    mushrooms,
    drained

Cut grouse in half and dust with flour. In a large skillet, melt the butter. Add grouse and brown on all sides. Add chicken broth and onions and bring broth to a gentle boil. Turn heat to low, cover, and simmer for 30 minutes.

With a slotted spoon, lift grouse pieces from skillet and place in a large greased ovenproof casserole. To the liquid in the skillet, add mushrooms; stir. In a small bowl, combine sherry, salt, pepper, cornstarch, and sour cream. Stir into the liquid in the skillet. Bring liquid to a boil, then pour over grouse in casserole. Cover and bake in a 325°F oven for 20 minutes, or until grouse meat is tender.

Serves 3 to 4.

Loon Lake Vinegar Pie

A light, tart-tasting pie, almost always mistaken for lemon meringue pie.

3 tbsp. cornstarch	**3 egg yolks**
1¾ cups sugar	**1 baked 9-inch pie**
1½ cups hot water	**crust**
4 tbsp. vinegar	**3 egg whites**
½ cup butter	**¼ tsp. cream of tartar**

In a saucepan, combine cornstarch and 1½ cups of the sugar. Stir in water, vinegar, and butter. Cook over medium heat until thick.

In a bowl, beat the egg yolks. Stir a small amount of the cooked sugar-cornstarch mixture into the yolks, then pour yolks into the saucepan. Cook for about 3 minutes, stirring constantly. Pour cooked mixture into pie shell and let cool.

In a separate bowl, beat egg whites with cream of tartar until the whites are frothy. Gradually beat in remaining ¼ cup sugar and beat until meringue is stiff and glossy. Spread meringue over pie, sealing to edge of crust. Bake in a 350°F oven for 5 minutes, or until meringue is lightly browned.

Makes one 9-inch pie.

Fiddleheads with Butter Sauce

This delicate fern with the earthy aroma is a traditional Canadian favourite.

4 cups fiddleheads
2 cups water
1 tsp. salt
¼ cup butter

¼ cup lemon juice
½ cup grated Parmesan
    cheese

Wash fiddleheads thoroughly. In a large pot, stir together water and salt. Add fiddleheads, cover, and bring to a boil. Boil for 5 minutes.

In a small saucepan, melt the butter. Stir in lemon juice and cheese and heat until cheese is melted.

Drain fiddleheads and transfer to a large serving bowl. Pour butter sauce over fiddleheads and toss. Serve immediately.

Serves 6.

Wild-Leek and Potato Soup

Wild leeks and onions are favourites of those who enjoy foraging the fields and woods for nature's bounty.

20 wild leeks
 5 medium potatoes
 3 cups cold water
 2 cups milk
 1 cup whipping (35%)
    cream

1 tsp. salt
½ tsp. pepper
1 tsp. caraway seed
¼ cup butter

Wash and clean leeks thoroughly. Cut into pieces, reserving a few tablespoons of green leaves for garnish. Wash, peel, and slice potatoes. In a large saucepan, place leeks, potatoes, and cold water. Bring water to a boil and cook until potatoes are tender. Remove from heat and mash leeks and potatoes together with their cooking liquid. Add milk, cream, salt, pepper, and caraway seed. Return saucepan to stove and heat gently, being careful not to let the cream boil. Pour into soup bowls; dot with butter and garnish with reserved chopped leek leaves.

Serves 6 to 8.

John's Rum-and-Raisin Pie

A rich company pie that says, "Bring on the vanilla ice cream."

1 cup brown sugar
3 tbsp. cornstarch
2 cups dark raisins
1⅓ cups cold water
⅓ cup fresh orange juice
2 tbsp. fresh lemon juice

2 tbsp. dark rum or 1 tsp. rum extract
½ cup broken walnuts
1 tbsp. butter
Pastry for a 9-inch lattice-top pie (see p. 95)

In a medium saucepan, combine brown sugar, cornstarch, raisins, water, orange juice, lemon juice, and rum. Cook over medium heat, stirring, until thickened. Remove from heat and stir in walnuts and butter.

Roll out pastry and line a 9-inch pie plate. Fill with cooked mixture. Cover with pastry strips criss-crossed to form a lattice pattern. Trim and flute edges. Bake in a 350°F oven for 30 minutes, or until crust is brown. Serve slightly warm.

Makes one 9-inch pie.

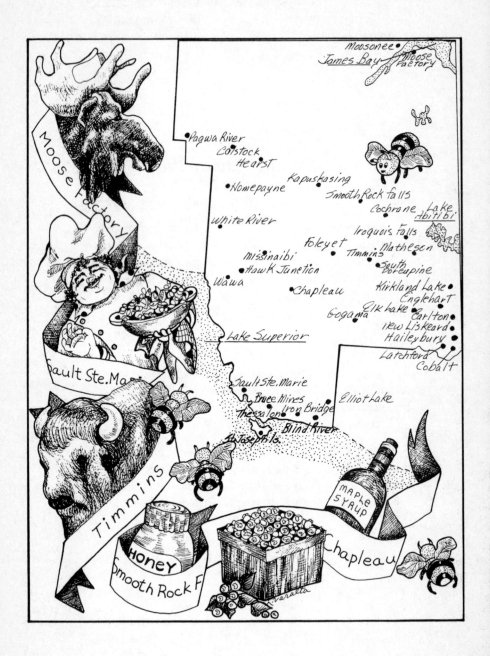

Moosonee
James Bay
Moose Factory

Moose Factory

Pagwa River
Calstock
Hearst
Kapuskasing
Homepayne
Smooth Rock falls
Cochrane   Lake Abitibi
White River
Iroquois Falls
Foleyet   Matheson
Missinaibi   Timmins
Hawk Junction   South Porcupine
Wawa
Chapleau   Kirkland Lake
Englehart
Gogama   Elk Lake
Carlton
New Liskeard
Haileybury
Lake Superior
Latchford
Cobalt

Sault Ste. Marie

Sault Ste. Marie
Bruce Mines
Thessalon   Iron Bridge   Elliot Lake
Blind River
St. Joseph Is.

Timmins

HONEY

Smooth Rock F.

MAPLE SYRUP

Chapleau

CHAPTER 9

ALL ROADS LEAD NORTH

*Scenic wilderness – mountains,
waterfalls, and forests. Travel by train to
the heart of the Agawa Canyon from the centre
of Sault Ste. Marie. It's a treasure trove for naturalists and
rock-hounds, and hunting for big game is a popular pastime
in the region. Wherever you go, there are hearty Italian
and Ukrainian traditional foods to eat, aptly suited for
this hardy climate.*

Recipes

Restaurants of the Region

BATCHEWANA BAY, SAULT STE. MARIE

Saltzburger Hof • Hearty German cooking and baking

KAPUSKASING

Dante's • Traditional Italian fare and home baking

Kapuskasing Inn • A quaint old hotel with a good dining room

MATHESON

Kiss Motel • Hungarian home-cooked delights and wonderful desserts

NEW LISKEARD

Breaults Motor Hotel • Steak, fresh fish, and home baking

RAMORE

The Lava Mountain • Exciting buffets and Sunday roast beef too

ROSSPORT

Rossport Inn • A 101-year-old inn with an excellent dining room offering Lake Superior whitefish and trout

SAULT STE. MARIE

Casari's • A large old-fashioned Italian restaurant

A Thymely Manner • Run with the enthusiasm and panache of two young people dedicated to the Italian culinary tradition. Sophisticated, delicious dining in a charming old house, a combination of old and new

TARSWELL, KIRKLAND LAKE

The Halfway House • Wonderful summer buffets; in winter, a hearty menu

THESSALON

The Farmhouse • Home baking and light meals adjacent to the Round Barn gift shop

Vitello Tonnato (Cold Veal with Tuna Sauce)

Sault Ste. Marie (known as "the Soo") sits on one of the most active canals in the St. Lawrence Seaway system. French missionaries established the city in 1669. Then steel, lumber, and shipping attracted a major Italian immigration, and Italian cuisine predominates in this pretty city. Some restaurants will prepare a take-out lunch for a day-trip on the Algoma Central train, which goes through the wilderness of Agawa Canyon. Near waterfalls, trout streams, and forests, you can enjoy a picnic of Vitello Tonnato or a cold pasta salad.

1 3½ lb. boneless
   rolled leg of veal
1 onion, chopped
2 cups dry white wine
¼ cup lemon juice

A few strips of
   lemon zest
2 bay leaves
¼ cup vegetable oil
1 quart water
1 bouquet garni
   (see Note)

Sauce

3 6½-oz. cans tuna,
   packed in oil, not
   drained
2 2-oz. cans anchovy
   fillets, drained
   and washed

3 cups mayonnaise
1 3½-oz. jar capers,
   drained
6 gherkins
1 lemon, cut in slices

In a large roasting pan, place veal, onion, wine, lemon juice, lemon zest, bay leaves, vegetable oil, water, and bouquet garni. Cover the pan, place over high heat, and bring liquids to a boil. Simmer for 2 hours, or until veal is tender.

Remove veal from roasting pan. Line a strainer with cheesecloth and set over a large saucepan. Strain cooking liquid through strainer and discard residue; place veal in strained cooking liquid and allow to cool. (Cooling in the liquid will intensify the flavour of the veal.)

When cooled, remove veal to a platter. Place saucepan with cooking liquid over high heat and bring liquid to a boil; cook until liquid is reduced by three-quarters.

To make sauce: Stir together tuna and anchovy fillets. With a wooden spoon, mash and pound anchovies until tuna and anchovies form a paste. Add a few tablespoons of reduced cooking liquid and mix thoroughly.

In a large bowl, pour mayonnaise. Add tuna-anchovy paste to mayonnaise a little at a time; stir until well blended.

Cut veal into very thin slices and layer on individual plates. Mask meat completely with sauce. Sprinkle each plate with a few capers; set a gherkin on each plate; garnish with lemon slices.

Serves 6.

Note: For bouquet garni, tie together, with string, 3 sprigs of parsley, 10 chives, 1 bay leaf, and 1 piece tarragon. Leave the string long enough to hang over the side of the saucepan. Or place ½ tsp. dried parsley, ½ tsp. tarragon, ½ tsp. thyme and 1 bay leaf on a square of cheesecloth. With string, tie into a small bag. (The bag can be dropped into the saucepan.)

Quail with Red Grape and Vermouth Sauce

These tiny birds are enhanced by the sunny flavours of northern Italy.

Stuffing

½ cup cooked rice
1 tsp. onion, minced
1 tbsp. celery, minced

1 small clove garlic, minced
Pinch of ground thyme
1 egg, beaten

Quail

6 2-oz. quail, boned (see Note)
Salt

Freshly ground black pepper
2 tbsp. oil
2 tbsp. butter

Grape and Vermouth Sauce

¼ cup red dry vermouth
12 to 15 seedless red grapes

¼ cup beef stock
Salt
Freshly ground black pepper

Combine rice, onion, celery, garlic, and thyme. Mix well. Stir in egg. Sprinkle quail with salt and pepper. Stuff each quail lightly with stuffing and close skin with wooden skewers.

In a skillet, melt oil and butter over high heat. Add quail and brown. Place skillet in a 400°F oven for 8 minutes. Remove quail and keep warm.

To make sauce: Pour oil from skillet. Return empty skillet to stove element. Add vermouth to skillet and scrape up bits from bottom and sides of pan. Add grapes and beef stock and simmer until sauce thickens slightly. Season to taste with salt and pepper. Pour over quail and serve immediately.

Serves 2.

Note: Ask butcher to bone quail, leaving wing and leg bones in the bird.

Caponata Sauce for Pasta

An Italian garden in a bowl.

¼ cup olive oil	¾ cup diced eggplant
2 tbsp. butter	1 medium green
2 ripe beefsteak	pepper, sliced
tomatoes, chopped	3 cloves garlic, minced
1 small red onion,	½ cup tomato sauce
chopped	Salt
½ cup diced zucchini	Pepper

In a large saucepan over medium heat, melt the olive oil and butter. Add tomatoes, onion, zucchini, eggplant, green pepper, and garlic and sauté for 8 to 10 minutes, or until vegetables are tender. Add the tomato sauce and simmer for 8 to 10 more minutes. Season with salt and pepper and serve hot over fresh pasta.

Serves 4 to 6.

Osso Buco

A traditional Italian family dish. The shank is an economical and tasty cut of meat.

Braised Veal Shank

6 meaty veal shin bones	Freshly ground black pepper
Salt	Flour
	¼ cup vegetable oil

Garnish

Minced fresh parsley	Pinch grated lemon peel

Sauce

1 tsp. olive oil	3 cloves garlic, minced
1 tbsp. butter	1 cup dry red wine
1 large onion, finely chopped	4 cups finely chopped tomatoes
1 medium carrot, chopped	1½ tsp. brown sugar
2 stalks celery, chopped	Salt
	Pepper

Season veal with salt and pepper and dust with flour. In a large skillet, heat oil. Add veal and sauté on all sides until meat is brown. In a casserole dish just large enough to contain the meat, set veal.

To make the sauce: In a second large skillet, heat olive oil and butter. Add onion and sauté until onion is soft. Add carrot, celery, and garlic and sauté over medium heat for 5 minutes. Stir in wine, tomatoes, and brown sugar and cook just until liquid starts to boil. Season with salt and pepper.

Pour sauce over veal and cover. Bake in a 350°F oven for 1 hour. Remove cover and bake for 30 minutes more, or until meat is tender.

Sprinkle with minced parsley and lemon peel.

Serves 6.

Red Pepper and Tomato Soup

The first amphibians and primitive land plants developed in the Devonian period of the earth's history. A short trip by freighter canoe will take you to Fossil Island, where you can see traces of this period. Be prepared for the cold. Cree Indians will build a fire on the island and serve bannock and tea to ward off the chill. It's not drawing-room style, but it's certainly authentic.

Winter nights start early this far north, and nothing warms you like a rich and tasty soup with the sunny flavours of autumn.

2 tbsp. butter	*Cayenne pepper*
1 tbsp. olive oil	*Bouquet garni*
3 large red onions,	*(see Note)*
thinly sliced	**6 cups canned plum**
6 large sweet red	*tomatoes, drained,*
peppers, seeded	*peeled, and*
and thinly sliced	*chopped*
6 large cloves garlic	**3 tbsp. dry sherry**
1 large carrot, diced	**1 tbsp. red wine**
1 tsp. dried thyme	*vinegar*
½ tsp. dried oregano	**5 cups chicken stock**
Salt	*Freshly ground pepper*

In a large saucepan over medium heat, melt butter with oil. Add onions and cook until onions begin to turn golden; do not brown. Stir in peppers, garlic, carrot, thyme, oregano, salt, and cayenne pepper. Add bouquet garni. Reduce heat to low, cover, and cook for 10 minutes, stirring occasionally. Add plum tomatoes, sherry, and vinegar, and cook, uncovered, stirring frequently, for 10 minutes. Stir in chicken stock. Bring liquid to a boil, then reduce heat and simmer for 10 minutes. Season to taste with pepper and serve immediately.

Serves 12.

Note: For bouquet garni: on a small square of cheesecloth, place 1 bay leaf, 4 celery leaves, 4 leek greens, 4 sprigs of parsley, and a 2-inch strip of orange peel. Bring corners of cheesecloth together to form a bag; tie neck of bag securely with kitchen string.

Warm Wilted Chard Salad

An uncommon vegetable makes this a sturdy and unusual salad.

1 bunch Swiss chard
1 bunch spinach,
   washed and
   chopped
2 medium zucchini,
   thinly sliced
1 medium red onion,
   sliced into thin
   rings
1 small cauliflower,
   cut into small
   flowerets

8 mushrooms, sliced
5 strips bacon, cut into
   small pieces
2 tbsp. red wine
   vinegar
3 tbsp. vegetable oil
1 tsp. sugar
1 tsp. dry mustard
2 medium carrots,
   grated
Toasted almonds

Wash the chard. Chop the leaves and cut the stalks into thin strips. In a large mixing bowl, combine the chard, spinach, zucchini, onion, cauliflower, and mushrooms. Set aside.

In a small frying pan, fry bacon until crispy. Remove bacon from the pan and drain. Crumble and set aside.

In a large frying pan or wok, combine vinegar, oil, sugar, and dry mustard. Over low heat, cook liquid until it bubbles. Add reserved vegetables to the frying pan and stir over low heat until chard and spinach begin to wilt. This will take no more than 2 minutes.

Place salad on a serving platter and garnish with crumbled bacon, grated carrots, and toasted almonds.

Serves 4.

Marinated Buffalo Roast

Time was when buffalo roamed this range. A buffalo roast, marinated and seasoned, can make an exciting meal on a stormy winter night. Now buffalo can be at home on your range. Kidd Creek Mines Limited in Timmins sells part of its herd to a local butcher. This tasty roast has 50 per cent fewer calories than beef and 30 per cent more protein.

¾ cup apple cider
¼ cup plus 2 tbsp.
   apple-cider
   vinegar
1 medium carrot, diced
1 medium onion, diced
1 celery stalk, diced
2 bay leaves
1 tsp. whole cloves
1 tsp. crushed juniper
   berries

1 small twig from a
   pine tree
   (thoroughly washed)
4 lbs. buffalo meat
   from neck or
   shoulder, trimmed
Salt
Pepper
2 tbsp. vegetable oil
⅜ cup all-purpose flour
¾ cup water

In a large bowl, stir together cider, vinegar, carrot, onion, celery, bay leaves, cloves, juniper berries, and pine twig. Add the buffalo meat, cover, and refrigerate for 4 to 5 days, turning the meat once a day.

Remove meat from marinade and season with salt and pepper.

In a large roasting pan, heat vegetable oil. Sear all sides of the meat until it is brown all over.

With a slotted spoon, remove vegetables and spices from marinade. Discard pine twig. Add to roasting pan and brown vegetables lightly. Add flour and stir, then stir in water and the marinade liquid. Cover the roasting pan and roast buffalo in a 350°F oven for about 1 hour and 30 minutes, turning meat every 20 minutes. If sauce is evaporating, fill pan with water to the original level.

Serves 6.

Note: This recipe can also be made with beef chuck or rump roast. Reduce marinating time to overnight.

Reindeer Steak with Pepper and Brandy Sauce

This is big-game country. Buffalo roasts and reindeer steaks sit next to veal shanks and pork tenderloin in the local butcher shops. This Scandinavian recipe for reindeer is enhanced by cracked peppercorns.

Reindeer

2 tsp. black pepper-
corns, coarsely
ground
4 loin or leg fillets of
reindeer

Salt
2 tbsp. olive oil or
vegetable oil

Sauce

¼ cup brandy
⅓ cup whipping (35%)
cream

½ tsp. crushed pepper-
corns
2 sprigs of watercress

With the heel of your hand, press coarsely ground peppercorns into reindeer fillets. Sprinkle fillets lightly with salt. In a large heavy skillet, heat olive oil over high heat. Add fillets and sear for 2 minutes on each side. Remove fillets and keep warm; turn heat to medium.

To make sauce: Pour brandy into skillet. Scrape up brown bits from bottom of skillet. Pour in whipping cream and stir in crushed peppercorns. Cook for 2 to 3 minutes. Pour hot sauce over fillets, garnish with watercress, and serve.

Serves 4.

Pork Tenderloin with Sauce Ste. Marie

A favourite dish in "the Soo."

Sauce

2 carrots
2 celery stalks
2 small onions
2 tbsp. vegetable oil
2 tbsp. ketchup

2 tbsp. Worcestershire
   sauce
1 tsp. sugar
Salt
Pepper
3 cups tomato juice

Pork

1 pork tenderloin,
   about 1¼ lbs.
1 egg
1 tsp. pepper

½ cup all-purpose flour
½ cup breadcrumbs
Oil

Chop carrots, celery, and onions. In a large skillet, heat oil. Add vegetables and fry over medium heat until vegetables are limp. Add ketchup, Worcestershire sauce, sugar, salt, and pepper. Pour in tomato juice and simmer for about 30 minutes, uncovered.

Meanwhile, slice pork-tenderloin strip into about eight 1-inch pieces. Place one piece, cut-side down, on a cutting board. With a wooden mallet, flatten the meat. Repeat for all pieces.

In a small bowl, beat the egg. Beat in pepper and flour; add breadcrumbs and mix thoroughly.

In a large skillet, over medium heat, heat the oil. Dip pieces of meat in egg-breadcrumb batter, then place in skillet. Cook 3 to 4 minutes on each side, or until meat is no longer pink.

Place pieces of meat on a serving platter. Spoon about 1 cup of sauce over the meat. Serve remaining sauce in sauce boat.

Serves 4.

Sweet-and-Sour Mooseballs

Many cultures settled in the north. The Ukrainian immigrants who arrived in 1891 brought recipes like cabbage rolls. They also adapted old-country recipes to suit a new environment – for example, sweet-and-sour mooseballs. A museum in Timmins marks the Ukrainians' contribution.

Mooseballs

1 ½ lbs. ground
    moosemeat
1 egg
1 medium onion,
    minced
1 ½ tsp. salt

¼ tsp. black pepper
1 clove garlic, minced
½ cup tomato sauce
1 cup breadcrumbs
Oil

Sauce

1 ½ cups beef stock
1 tbsp. cornstarch
3 tbsp. brown sugar
1 tbsp. vinegar

1 tbsp. mustard
½ cup tomato sauce
Parsley

In a large mixing bowl, combine ground moosemeat, egg, and minced onion. Stir in salt, pepper, and garlic. Add tomato sauce and breadcrumbs and mix well with your hands. Form the mixture into small balls, each about 1 inch in diameter.

In a large frying pan, heat oil. Add meatballs and cook until meat is tender, about 20 minutes, turning meatballs occasionally. Remove from heat. With a slotted spoon, lift out meatballs.

Drain fat from frying pan. Pour beef stock into frying pan and bring stock to a boil.

In a small bowl, combine cornstarch, brown sugar, vinegar, mustard, and tomato sauce. Add mixture to beef stock, mixing thoroughly, and bring to the boil again. Reduce heat until liquid is simmering, then add cooked mooseballs.

Simmer for a few minutes to heat meatballs through. Serve garnished with parsley.

Serves 6 to 8.

Note: To derive the fullest flavour from the moose, prepare the dish a day ahead. As dish sits, the flavours of the ingredients mingle and develop.

Roast Moose in Beer

The Company of Adventurers, from England, settled Moosonee and Moose Factory. The two towns huddle next to the icy waters of James Bay. Big game is the staple, and most homemakers fill the freezer with the fruits of their fall hunt to tide them over the winter.

3 lbs. moose (blade,
cross-rib, or rump
roast)
½ cup all-purpose flour
Salt

Pepper
2 bay leaves
2 Spanish onions, sliced
1 bottle dark beer

Set the roast in the freezer for about 2 hours, to make it easier to slice. Cut the meat across the grain into quarter-inch slices. In a baking dish with a cover or in a slow cooker, arrange 2 layers of meat slices. (You should use about one-third of the meat.) In a small bowl, stir together flour, salt, and pepper. Sprinkle half the seasoned flour over the meat slices. Add bay leaves. Arrange half the onion slices over the bay leaves. Then add a layer of meat; sprinkle with seasoned flour; add remaining onions and finish with remaining meat slices. Pour the beer over the meat.

Cover the baking dish and bake in a 350°F oven for 2 hours and 30 minutes; or cook in a covered slow cooker for 8 hours. Do not uncover roast during cooking.

Serves 8.

Marinated Bear Steaks

This is the closest you should ever get to a bear.

4 bear steaks, 1 ¼ to
   1 ½ inches thick
1 onion, sliced
½ cup red wine vinegar
½ cup olive oil
1 clove garlic, smashed

1 tbsp. pickling spice
½ cup water
Oil
Salt
Pepper

Trim all fat from steaks. Discard fat; wash steaks well in cold water. In a large glass bowl, combine onion, vinegar, olive oil, garlic, pickling spice, and water. Place steaks in marinade and marinate for at least 24 hours in the refrigerator, turning steaks from time to time.

The next day, remove steaks from marinade. Drain and pat dry. Using just enough oil to prevent steaks from sticking, pan-fry the steaks, turning occasionally, for 15 to 20 minutes. Season with salt and freshly ground pepper. Serve immediately.

Serves 4.

Ukrainian Cabbage Rolls

These will warm your heart on a winter eve.

1 lb. ground beef
¼ cup uncooked rice
1 egg
1 onion, grated
1 carrot, grated
¼ tsp. salt

12 cabbage leaves
¼ cup lemon juice
½ cup brown sugar
1 cup tomato sauce
1 cup raisins

In a large bowl, combine meat, rice, and egg. Stir in onion, carrot, and salt. Set aside. In a saucepan, cover cabbage leaves with boiling water. Boil for 2 to 3 minutes; drain.

Place a ball of the meat-and-rice mixture in the centre of each cabbage leaf and roll up the leaf. Tuck in the ends securely. In a heavy frying pan with a tight-fitting lid, set rolls close together. Add lemon juice, brown sugar, tomato sauce, and raisins. Pour in enough water to cover the cabbage rolls. Cover tightly and cook over moderate heat for 30 minutes. Reduce heat and simmer for 20 minutes more.

Place frying pan in a 350°F oven and bake, uncovered, for 20 minutes, or until rolls are brown. Turn cabbage rolls once to brown evenly. Add hot water while baking if liquid evaporates.

Serves 6.

Green Tomato Pie

Green tomatoes still on the vine when Jack Frost is on the prowl? Bake them in a pie!

*Pastry for a 2-crust
9-inch pie (see
page 95)
3 tbsp. all-purpose
flour
1¼ cups sugar
1 tsp. salt
½ tsp. nutmeg*

*½ tsp. cinnamon
1 tsp. lemon rind
3 cups thinly sliced
green tomatoes
3 tbsp. lemon juice or
vinegar
1 tbsp. butter or
margarine*

Roll out pastry and line a 9-inch pie plate with crust.

Combine flour, sugar, salt, nutmeg, cinnamon, and lemon rind. Sprinkle bottom crust with half the flour-sugar mixture. Arrange the green tomatoes in the crust, then sprinkle with remaining flour-sugar mixture. Sprinkle lemon juice or vinegar over pie; dot with butter or margarine.

Add top crust, sealing the edges, and bake in a 450°F oven for 10 minutes. Reduce heat to 350°F and bake for 45 minutes more, or until crust is golden brown.

Makes one 9-inch pie.

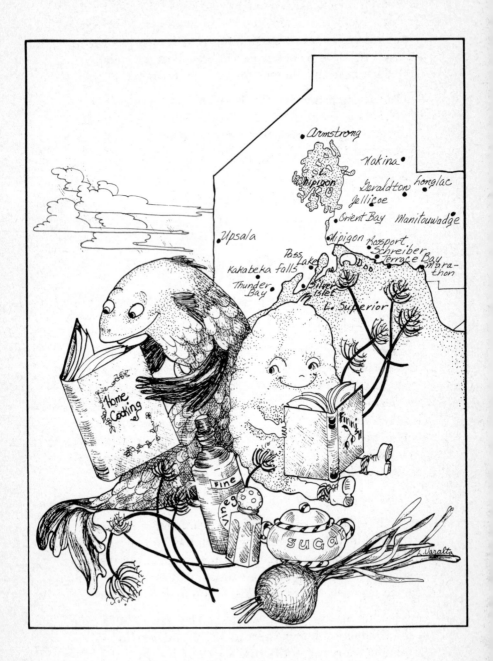

Armstrong

Nakina

St. hipigon

Beraldton honglac

Jellicoe

Orient Bay Manitouwadge

Upsala

dipigon Rossport

Schreiber

Pass. Terrace Bay

Kakabeka falls Lake Marathon

Thunder Bob

Bay Silver

Islet

L. Superior

Home Cooking

Fine Veg

Suga

L. Varalta

210

CHAPTER 10

NORTH OF SUPERIOR

*Mount McKay, the home of the
legendary Ojibwa "Great Spirit," offers
a wonderful vista and a new appreciation of
magnificent lakes and forests. In Old Fort William, an
unparalleled reconstruction of life 170 years ago, you
can taste the foods of the voyageurs. And in the city of
Thunder Bay, there are traditional dishes brought by
the Finnish and Slavic settlers, who felt at home in this
northern region. Generations later, the recipes are still
prepared in the same old-country ways.*

Recipes

Restaurants of the Region

GERALDTON

The Park Bay View Motel • Straightforward home-cooked meals

THUNDER BAY

Airline Motor Hotel • Good dining room

Harrington Court • Chicken and fish are house specialties

Hoito Restaurant • A large, plain family restaurant serving hearty home-style Finnish fare

Kanga's Sauna • A coffee shop and public sauna with Finnish home cooking

La Torre Dining Lounge • Traditional cuisine

Old Fort William • An excursion into history. Here is delicious Canadian frontier cooking in a cafeteria-style dining room

Old Fort William Bread

Old Fort William is a monument to Thunder Bay's early days. In the dining hall you'll find Scottish currant scones, which were enjoyed by the early fur traders, on the same menu as French-Canadian pea soup, which was eaten by the trappers. The old fort, with its many public and private buildings, has been completely rebuilt. Every detail is faithful to the past.

1 tsp. sugar	4 tbsp. sugar
1 cup lukewarm water	1½ tsp. salt
1 package yeast	½ cup lard or
3 cups stone-ground	shortening
flour	2 cups warm water
4 cups unbleached	
white flour	

Dissolve the 1 tsp. sugar in 1 cup lukewarm water. Stir in yeast and let stand for 10 minutes.

Meanwhile, in a very large bowl, stir together stone-ground flour and unbleached white flour. Stir in the 4 tbsp. sugar and the salt. Using your fingers, rub lard into flour until mixture is smooth. Stir yeast mixture and add to flour; pour in remaining 2 cups warm water. Mix well.

Turn dough out onto a well-floured board and knead until smooth. (This will take about 10 minutes.) Place dough in a large greased bowl and turn once to grease top. Cover and let rise in a warm, draft-free place until dough has doubled in bulk, about 1 hour and 30 minutes. Punch dough down and form into 2 loaves. Place loaves in greased 8 by 4-inch loaf pans. Cover the loaves and let rise in a warm, draft-free spot for about 1 hour, or until doubled in bulk.

Bake in a 350°F oven for 30 to 40 minutes, or until loaves sound hollow when tapped on top and bottom. Cool on racks.

Makes two 1-lb. loaves.

Molasses Bread

This tawny brown bread has a memorable rich, sweet taste.

2 cups lukewarm water
½ cup butter
½ tsp. salt
½ cup plus 1 tsp. sugar

1 cup molasses
8 cups all-purpose flour
1 package yeast

In a large pot, pour 1¾ cups of the water. Add butter. Heat, stirring, till butter melts. Add salt and ½ cup of the sugar. Stir till sugar is dissolved. Stir in molasses. Slowly add 1 cup of the flour and mix well with an electric beater or hand egg beater. Let stand for 20 minutes.

Meanwhile, dissolve remaining 1 tsp. sugar in remaining ¼ cup warm water. Stir in yeast and let stand for about 10 minutes.

Transfer molasses mixture to a large bowl. Add yeast mixture. Add remaining 7 cups of flour, one cup at a time, beating well after each addition; when dough is too stiff to beat, turn it out onto a lightly floured board and work in the rest of the flour with your hands. Knead dough for about 10 minutes, or until it feels elastic. Place dough in a flour-dusted bowl and sprinkle the top with flour; let rise for about 1 hour, or until it has doubled in bulk.

Punch dough down and shape into 3 loaves. Place each loaf in a buttered 8 by 4-inch loaf pan. Let rise in a warm, draft-free place until doubled in bulk, about 1 hour. Bake in a 300°F oven for 45 to 55 minutes, or until loaves sound hollow when tapped. Cool on racks.

Makes 3 loaves.

Old Fort William Pea Soup

A bowl of this "stick-to-the-ribs" soup is a good defence against below-zero weather.

1 lb. split peas	¼ tsp. ground savory
½ lb. salt pork	6 whole cloves
1 meaty ham bone	1½ tsp. salt
2 medium onions, diced	¼ tsp. pepper
¾ cup diced carrots	1 tbsp. chopped parsley
1 tsp. dry mustard	

In a large kettle, cover peas with water; then add 4 inches more water. Add salt pork, ham bone, onions, and carrots; stir in mustard, savory, cloves, salt, and pepper. Bring liquid to a boil, then reduce heat immediately. Simmer gently for about 2 hours and 30 minutes, or until peas are tender.

Season to taste, sprinkle with parsley, and serve immediately.

Serves 8.

Fresh Salted Salmon in Dill (Vahansuolattu Lohi)

North of Lake Superior is Thunder Bay, the cradle of the Canadian fur trade. Early settlers were mainly Scots. Now, among others, there is a large Finnish community, which has influenced and enlivened the local cuisine. Gravlax, a special favourite, can be made in the refrigerator; no cooking is required.

3 tbsp. coarse salt	2 fresh salmon fillets,
3 tbsp. sugar	1 lb. each, with
1½ tbsp. coarsely	skin
crushed pepper-	½ cup tightly packed
corns	coarsely chopped
	fresh dill

In a small bowl, combine salt, sugar, and crushed peppercorns; reserve.

On a work surface, place salmon fillets skin-side up. Scrape the edge of a large sharp knife over the salmon skin three or four times, wiping the blade of the knife clean with a paper towel each time. Wipe salmon skin clean with a damp paper towel. Turn salmon flesh-side up and run your hand over fish to feel for small bones; remove with tweezers.

In a glass baking dish just large enough to hold the salmon in 2 layers, place one salmon fillet, skin-side down. Rub half the salt-sugar mixture into salmon flesh; sprinkle with ¼ cup of the chopped dill. Rub remaining salt-sugar mixture into flesh of second fillet. Place second salmon fillet on top of the first, skin-side-up, fitting thick side to thin side. Sprinkle with remaining ¼ cup dill. Cover baking dish loosely with plastic wrap, then place a small carving board or plate on top of the salmon fillets. Top with weights. (You might use 2 large unopened cans.) Refrigerate for 48 hours, turning salmon fillets once every 12 hours and draining off any liquid that accumulates.

Before serving, scrape salt-sugar mixture and dill off salmon fillets. With a long, sharp, thin-bladed knife, carefully remove salmon skin; discard. To serve, cut salmon in thin diagonal slices.

Serves 8.

Finnish Sirloin-Tip Pot Roast (Linnanpaisti)

A decidedly different pot roast with an aromatic, pungent gravy.

1 tbsp. butter
1 tbsp. vegetable oil
3 lbs. boneless sirloin tip
1 Spanish onion, coarsely chopped
Salt
Freshly ground pepper
1 1¾-oz. can anchovy fillets, drained, rinsed, and patted dry
2 tbsp. red wine vinegar

2 tbsp. brandy
1½ tbsp. molasses
1 tsp. whole allspice
1 bay leaf
½ tsp. whole peppercorns
1½ to 2 cups beef stock, or as needed
1 tbsp. cornstarch
½ cup whipping (35%) cream

In a roasting pan or a Dutch oven, melt together butter and oil. Add meat and cook, turning to brown all sides. (This will take about 10 minutes.) Remove meat from roasting pan and add onions; brown. Return roast to pan and sprinkle lightly with salt and pepper. Add anchovies, vinegar, brandy, molasses, allspice, bay leaf, and peppercorns to pan; add stock to halfway up the side of the roast.

Cook, covered, over low heat until roast is fork-tender, about 3 hours, basting and turning meat frequently. Add stock as necessary to maintain level of liquid. Remove roast from pan and set on a serving platter. Strain the cooking liquid into a saucepan. (You should have 1½ to 2 cups.) Skim fat from surface. Set gravy over medium heat and heat to simmering. While gravy is heating, in a small bowl, combine cornstarch and whipping cream; stir into simmering gravy. Heat gravy over medium-high heat, stirring constantly, for about 5 minutes, being careful not to boil the cream. Cut roast into thin slices and serve immediately with gravy.

Serves 6.

Shoemaker's Salmon (Suutarinlohi)

Just as the shoemaker's children don't always get shoes, so the salmon fisher's children don't always get salmon.

1 lb. small fresh smelts, dressed	**⅔ cup finely chopped onion**
1½ tsp. coarse salt	**½ cup water**
1⅓ cup white wine vinegar	**2 tsp. sugar**
	½ tsp. crushed allspice

In a glass baking dish, place smelts, skin-side down. (You should have only 1 layer of smelts.) Sprinkle smelts with salt.

In a small saucepan, stir together vinegar, onion, water, sugar, and allspice. Set marinade over medium heat and simmer for 5 minutes.

Pour hot marinade over fish. Cover and refrigerate for 2 days. Lift smelts from marinade; with a slotted spoon, lift onion from marinade.

Serve smelts whole with a garnish of marinated onions and buttered dark bread.

Serves 6 as an appetizer.

Note: If you use frozen smelts, make sure they are thoroughly thawed.

This dish is also good made with 1 tsp. honey instead of the sugar.

Herring Salad (Sillisalatti)

A traditional Finnish dish that will add zest to your salad bar.

3 medium beets
3 medium carrots
3 medium potatoes
1 small onion, chopped
¼ cup chopped sweet
   pickles

1 medium salt herring
   (about 1½ lbs.)
2 or 3 hard-cooked
   eggs, chopped

In separate pots, cook unpeeled beets, carrots, and potatoes until tender. Drain. When vegetables are cool, peel and dice. (You should have about 1½ cups of beets and carrots and about 1 cup of potatoes.) In a large bowl, place diced vegetables; add onion and sweet pickles.

Wash salt herring in cold water and remove skin and bones. Dice herring meat and add to vegetables. Toss all ingredients together lightly and let stand in the refrigerator for 3 hours. To serve, sprinkle with chopped eggs.

Serves 6.

Note: This salad is very tasty with a dash of vinegar.

Beef Rolls with Gravy (Zraziki Po Krakowsku)

Delicious Polish meals—like beef rolls with gravy—are still prepared by methods brought from the old country. These beef rolls add a piquant touch of pickle to a traditional Polish repast.

1½ to 2 lbs. round steak
Salt
Pepper
1 onion, finely chopped
¼ cup butter
1 cup breadcrumbs
1 tsp. minced parsley
1 egg, beaten
1 tbsp. pickle relish
1 cup all-purpose flour
1 cup hot water or beef stock
Parsley

Pound meat until it is about three-eighths inch thick, then cut into pieces, each about 3 by 4 inches. Season with salt and pepper.

In a small skillet, sauté onion in 1 tbsp. of the butter until onion is transparent. Add breadcrumbs, parsley, egg, salt, pepper, and relish. Remove from heat and mix well. Spread about 2 tbsp. of the onion mixture on each meat slice and roll meat tightly. Tie securely with string or fasten with toothpicks. Roll meat rolls in flour.

In a large skillet, melt remaining butter. Add meat rolls and sauté until brown, turning to cook all sides. Add hot water or beef stock and simmer for about 1 hour and 30 minutes. With a slotted spoon, lift meat rolls from the skillet. Remove string or toothpicks and arrange rolls on a serving platter. Pour gravy over meat, garnish with parsley, and serve immediately.

Serves 6 to 8.

Note: These are delicious served with mashed potatoes.

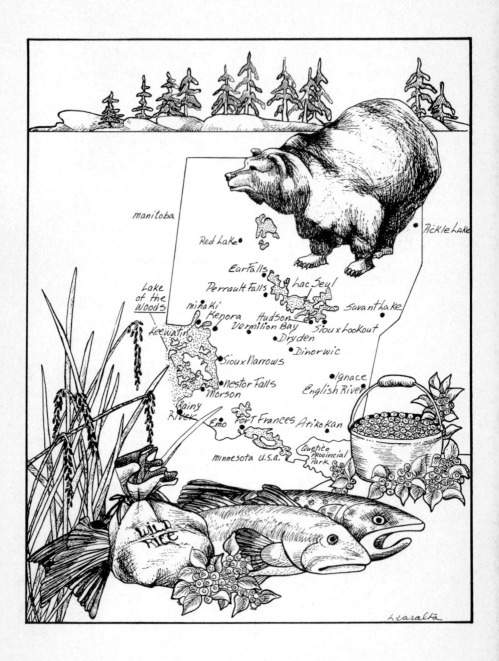

manitoba

Red Lake

EarFalls
Perrault Falls   Lac Seul

Lake
of the   Minaki
Woods   Kenora   Hudson   Savant Lake
                              Vermilion Bay
Keewatin   Sioux Lookout
                              Dryden
                              Dinorwic

                  Sioux Narrows
                                    Ignace
            Nestor Falls   English River
            Morson

Rainy
River   Emo   Fort Frances Atikokan

      Minnesota U.S.A.   Quetico
                              Provincial
                              Park

Pickle Lake

WILD RICE

L. Varalta

CHAPTER 11

SUNSET COUNTRY

In a land once travelled by canoe,
one can see a grandeur never before
imagined. There's a sense of peace in the rugged
beauty that prevails in this northern wilderness. Pick wild
berries, fish for "the big ones," or just breathe deeply and
enjoy the view.

Recipes

Restaurants of the Region

DRYDEN

Lindemeirs Lodge • At this luxurious drive-in fishing lodge the impressive pine dining room hangs right over the water. Bread six inches high and thickly sliced, enormous portions, and delicious meals make it worth the trip

KENORA

The Steak House • A cheerful steak house with salad bar, traditionally good

Travel Inn • The liveliest spot in Kenora with a good dining room, too

MINAKI

Minaki Lodge • Had it not been for the building of the transcontinental railway, Minaki Lodge might never have been constructed. Although renowned for its international cuisine, Minaki Lodge makes a specialty of presenting the game and fish of the area in an awesomely beautiful setting

Hot Pickerel and Wild-Rice Salad

Early settlers in Sioux Lookout prepared their daily catch in this simple manner. A century later, the dish is a gourmet's delight.

Rice

1 cup wild rice	1 tsp. salt
1 tbsp. butter	2½ cups water
1 tbsp. minced onion	

Fish

½ cup all-purpose flour	1 lb. fresh pickerel
½ tsp. baking powder	fillets
½ tsp. salt	Salt
¼ cup milk	Pepper
¼ cup water	Oil for deep frying

Wash rice thoroughly two or three times and remove any foreign particles; drain. In a saucepan with a tight-fitting lid, over medium heat, melt the butter. Add onion and sauté until onion is tender. Stir in rice and salt; add water and bring liquid to a boil, stirring occasionally. Reduce heat to low, cover, and cook without stirring for 40 to 50 minutes, or until liquid is absorbed.

While rice is cooking, prepare fish. In a small bowl, sift together flour, baking powder, and salt. Stirring constantly, slowly add milk and water; beat until batter is smooth. Set batter aside.

Cut pickerel fillets into small pieces–about 1-inch squares. Season fish pieces with salt and pepper, then dip in batter. Place fish in a frying basket and deep-fry until golden brown, about 4 to 5 minutes. Drain on paper towels and set aside until rice is ready.

When rice is boiled, transfer to a shallow buttered baking dish. Bake in a 250°F oven for 10 to 15 minutes, or until rice grains separate. Remove from oven and add fried-fish pieces. Toss and serve immediately.

Serves 6.

Wild-Rice Pancakes

Anglers and fishers are familiar with the luxurious fly-in and drive-in big-game fishing camps. But the camps seem to have been kept secret from us – most guests are American sportsmen. Kenora and Lake of the Woods offer placidly beautiful experiences. You can cruise the 14,500 islands of this unspoiled region, nibbling on fresh berries plucked from the shore. Native harvesters in canoes glide silently though the reeds gathering the wild rice that graces our Thanksgiving tables.

¼ cup wild rice
½ tsp. salt
2 tbsp. butter
2 cups all-purpose flour
2 tbsp. sugar
2 tsp. baking powder
1 tsp. baking soda

1 tsp. salt
2 eggs
2 cups buttermilk
Maple syrup or Wild-Blueberry Sauce (recipe follows)

Wash wild rice under cold running water. Stir rice into ¾ cup boiling water. Boil for 5 minutes, then remove from heat and let rice soak in the water, covered, for 1 hour. Drain and rinse.

Stir rice into 1½ cups boiling salted water. Cook until soft and partially puffed, about 15 minutes. Drain rice, pour it into a bowl, and add butter.

In a separate bowl, sift together flour, sugar, baking powder, baking soda, and salt.

In a large bowl, beat eggs until light. Stir in buttermilk. Add the flour mixture and beat until smooth. Stir in cooked rice.

Lightly grease a griddle and preheat. Drop batter by spoonfuls onto the griddle. When nicely browned on one side, turn the pancakes. Serve with butter, maple syrup, or Wild-Blueberry Sauce.

Serves 6.

Wild-Blueberry Sauce

2 cups fresh wild
  blueberries
¼ tsp. salt
1 cup water

¾ cup sugar
2 tbsp. cornstarch
1 tbsp. lemon juice

In a saucepan, combine blueberries, salt, and ¾ cup of the water. In a small bowl, combine sugar and cornstarch. Add remaining ¼ cup water and stir until smooth. Stir cornstarch mixture into blueberry mixture. Heat until liquid begins to boil. Reduce heat and simmer until sauce thickens and becomes clear. Stir in lemon juice. Serve hot or cold with pancakes.

Makes 2½ cups.

Note: Sauce can also be made with frozen blueberries. Thaw the berries before making the sauce.

Frozen Blueberry Soufflé

An exciting finish to a blueberry-picking expedition. Adapted from an original recipe to suit home cooking.

3 cups blueberries	**2 egg yolks**
¾ cup sugar	**Pinch salt**
1½ tbsp. orange juice	**½ tsp. grated orange**
1½ cups whipping (35%)	**rind**
cream	**2 tbsp. brandy**
3 eggs	**Icing sugar**

In a blender, purée blueberries. Add sugar and orange juice to the blender and mix well. In a small pot, bring berry purée to a boil; reduce heat and simmer until mixture is reduced to 1½ cups.

While purée is cooking, whip the cream until stiff; chill in refrigerator.

In a large bowl, stir together eggs and egg yolks, salt, and orange rind. Beat until batter is pale yellow and forms a ribbon when a spoonful is lifted. Slowly start adding hot berry purée to the batter, beating quickly all the time. Continue beating until the batter is cool, then beat in brandy. When batter is completely cooled, fold in chilled whipped cream. Spoon the batter into a 3-cup soufflé mould with a collar (see Note). Cover the mould with a sheet of plastic wrap. Freeze the soufflé for at least 6 hours.

To serve, let the soufflé stand at room temperature for 5 minutes, then gently remove plastic wrap and collar. Sprinkle soufflé with icing sugar.

Serves 6 to 8.

Note: To make a collar, cut a piece of parchment paper or heavy aluminum foil to 1⅓ times the circumference of the soufflé dish, and twice as high. Wrap the paper around the dish and secure the top with a paper clip. Tie kitchen string around the collar just below the rim of the dish.

Family-Size Blueberry, Raspberry, and Saskatoon-Berry Pie

A three-berry pie composed during a camping trip. Summer is the time to freeze a variety of berries; in winter, memories are rekindled with this luscious treat.

Pastry for a 2-crust
9-inch pie (see
page 95)
2 tsp. minute tapioca
2 cups fresh blueberries
1 cup fresh raspberries
1 cup fresh Saskatoon
berries

1 tbsp. lemon juice
¾ cup plus 1 tbsp.
sugar
4 tbsp. all-purpose
flour
½ tsp. cinnamon
2 tbsp. melted butter
1 tbsp. milk

Line a 9-inch pie plate with pastry. Sprinkle minute tapioca over the pastry. (The tapioca soaks up excess juice from the berries.)

In a large bowl, stir together blueberries, raspberries, Saskatoon berries, and lemon juice. Add ¾ cup of the sugar; stir in the flour, cinnamon, and melted butter. Pour into pie plate. Cover pie with top crust and cut a few slashes in the top. Seal edges well and flute. Brush crust lightly with milk and sprinkle with remaining 1 tbsp. sugar. Bake in a 425°F oven for 15 minutes, then reduce heat to 350°F and bake for about 40 minutes longer, or until crust is golden brown.

Makes one 9-inch pie.

Note: You can substitute 2 tbsp. cornstarch for the 4 tbsp. flour.

This pie is also quite good without the cinnamon.

Kenora Caboose

A caboose is a cabin on wheels at the end of a railway train where the conductor can relax. This drink, a favourite in Kenora, is a relaxing way to end a meal.

1 oz. vodka	**½ cup orange juice**
1 oz. pear liqueur	**1 maraschino cherry**
Ice	

Pour vodka and pear liqueur into a cocktail glass over ice. Add orange juice.

Garnish with a maraschino cherry.

Makes 1 cocktail.

That's Ontario—an exciting amalgam of past, present, and future. I'll see you there.

Sara Waxman

Entertaining
with
Wine and Cheese

*Like love and marriage, wine and cheese
complement each other so beautifully that they can
be used to create a warm and hospitable ambience.
I've compiled a table of Ontario cheeses and wines
that may be used compatibly.*

The Cheeses

• Serve salt-free water biscuits, crackers, or crusty French bread. These will not overpower the subtle taste of the cheese. Chèvre is excellent with classic English digestive biscuits. Strong-tasting cheese is mellowed by crackers or bread spread with unsalted butter.

• Allow lots of space on several cheese boards. Crowding is uncomfortable for the cheese and for the taster.

• Group appropriate cheeses and wines together. Choose a variety of shapes, colours, and flavour strengths.

• A bowl of fruit makes an edible centrepiece. Dried fruits are wonderful with port and sherry; apples go with everything; and ripe pears, grapes, plums, and cherries are a natural accompaniment for cheese. For variety, arrange crunchy vegetables with the fruit: celery, carrot, and rutabaga are delightful with Cheddar and other hard cheeses.

• Serve cheese at room temperature. Set up the table at least two hours in advance.

• Each cheese should have its own knife to prevent mixing of flavours.

The Wines

• Keep your selection of wines small.

• Ports and sherries with their corresponding cheeses, fresh pears, and walnuts in the shell make an interesting and sophisticated dessert menu.

• Champagnes and sparkling wines served with fresh strawberries, warm blanched almonds, an appropriate creamy cheese, and dark chocolate morsels make a spring wine-tasting exciting. Refrigerate champagne one day before serving. (Do not place it in the freezer for twenty minutes expecting that this will do the job. It bruises the delicate wine.) Serve champagne in flutes or tulip-shaped glasses. Just for fun have a "blind tasting." Serve champagne in one glass and sparkling wine in another. See who can tell the difference. The easiest way to open a bottle of champagne is gently. After you have unwrapped the neck of the bottle turn the cork in one direction and the bottle in the opposite direction.

• It is a good idea not to mix whites and reds in one tasting. But if you choose to do so serve the whites first then have an intermission, a palate cleansing, before you go on to the reds.

• At a white-wine and cheese party compare different brands and/or years of Chardonnays, Gewürtztraminers, or Rieslings. White wines should be chilled three to four hours in advance of serving. Often if they are ice cold, the full flavour cannot be appreciated.

• At a wine tasting allow six to eight glasses per bottle; at a wine and cheese party allow half a bottle per person.

• Red wines are wonderful with cheese. They should be served at room temperature. Beaujolais is often served slightly chilled. There are two methods. The wine may be prepoured and served or it may be poured at table. (Remember that red wine stains a mahogany table as well as a cloth. Lay several thicknesses of newspaper between your cloth and table.) The tablecloth should be white so that the colour and clarity of the wine may be clearly seen. For pouring at table, place the bottle of red wine on a tray with the glasses. Spills usually occur around the bottle. After red wine, most people will want coffee. Have it available with cookies, dainties, or large fruit pies.

• Table layouts are important. A square table could accommodate a grouping of wine and glasses at each corner, in the centre the cheese and fruit.

• Accessories to wine tasting are: pitchers of ice water and glasses; wine glass rinsers, for smaller groups cereal bowls for individual rinsing are suitable, and for larger groups a rinsing bucket such as an ice bucket or a large stainless-steel mixing bowl are adequate. Make sure that you have a good supply of luncheon-size paper napkins on hand, because after your guests rinse their empty glass they'll want to dry the outside before using it again.

CHEESE	WINE

Goat Cheese Chèvre
Fresh Chèvre
(Herbed, Peppered)
Mild Chèvre
Chèvre with Caraway Seeds
Feta
Aged Chèvre
Small cubes in olive oil
  with Italian herbs

Barnes Wines Limited
Limited Edition 1983 Pinot
  Chardonnay (White)

Inniskillin
Gamay Noir (Red)
Chelois (Red)

Brights
Entre-Lacs (White)
President Sherry

Chateau-Gai
Chateau-Gai 1982 Chardonnay
  (White)
Chateau-Gai 1982 Villard Noir
  (Red)

Chateau des Charmes
Aligore Estate (White)
Pinot Noir Nokara Estate (Red)

Hillebrand
Chardonnay 1982 (White)
Etienne Brulé Rouge (Red)

Soft
Anfleur
Buttiri
Casata
Alpina
Mozzarella
Serra
Butter
Brine Cured Brick

Barnes Wines
Heritage Estates Canadian
  Burgundy (Red)
LaCoste Sparkling White Wine

Inniskillin
Chardonnay (White)
Brae Blanc (White)
Brae Rouge (Red)

CHEESE	WINE

Soft
Anfleur
Buttiri
Casata
Alpina
Mozzarella
Serra
Butter
Brine Cured Brick

Brights
L'Entre Cote (White)
Riesling (White)
Gewürztraminer (White)
Chardonnay (White)
L'Entre Cote (Red)
Baco Noir (Red)
President Champagne (Sparkling)
President Brut Champagne
  (Sparkling)
President Sherry
Dry Sherry

Chateau-Gai
1982 Chardonnay (White)
LaMont Premium Blend Brut
  Sparkling White Wine

Chateau des Charmes
Estate Auxerrois (White)
Gamay Blanc (White)
Gamay Beaujolais Nouveau
  (Red)
Entrenous (Red)

Andres
Kurhauser Trocken Sekt
  (Sparkling)

Hillebrand
Gewürztraminer (White)

Podamer
Podamer Brut (Sparkling)
Podamer Brut Blanc de Blancs
  (Sparkling)
Podamer Extra Dry (Sparkling)

CHEESE	WINE

Creamy
Brie
Limburger
Le Baron
Bonne Mere
Camembert
Belle Creme
Caciotta

Inniskillin
Millot-Chamburtin (white)
Late Harvest Vidal (white)

Brights
Chardonnay (White)
Baco Noir (Red)
President Champagne (Sparkling)
President Cream Sherry
President Port

Chateau-Gai
1982 Chancellor (Red)
Hallmark Port
Hallmark Cream Sherry
Oloroso Sherry

Andres
Boisseau Blanc de Blancs
  (White)
Domain D'Or (White)
Botticelli (White)

Hillebrand
Johannisburg Riesling 1982
  (White)
Schloss Hillebrand (White)

Podamer
Podamer Brut (Sparkling)
Podamer Brut Blanc de Blancs
  (Sparkling)
Podamer Extra Dry (Sparkling)

CHEESE	WINE

Semi-soft
Monterey
Blue
Munster
Esrom
Oka
Havarti
Saint Paulin
Anfrom

Barnes Wines
Ontario Country Red
Springwood Canadian Sauterne
  (White)
Heritage Ruby Port

Inniskillin
Leon Millot Port

Brights
Chardonnay (White)
Gewürztraminer (White)
Baco Noir (Red)
Spumante (Sparkling)
President Champagne (Sparkling)
President Port
President Sherry

Chateau-Gai
1982 Villard Noir (Red)

Chateau des Charmes
Estate Riesling (1981) (White)
Primeur Rouge (Red)
Estate Chardonnay (White)
Pinot Noir Estate (Red)

Andres
Gold shield (White)
Wintergarten (White)
Hochtaler (White)
Botticelli (White)

Podamer
Concerto (White)

Reif
Riesling (White)
Vidal (White)

CHEESE	WINE

Soft Fresh Cream Cheese
Ricotta
Quark
Feta
Cottage

Inniskillin
Vidal (White)

Brights
LiebesHeim (White)
Riesling (White)
Spumante (Sparkling)
74 Port
74 Sherry
Cream Sherry

Chateau-Gai
1982 Johannisberg Riesling
   (White)
1982 Chancellor

Hard
Provolette
Swiss
Provolone
Gouda
Cacciocavallo
Scamorza
Tilsit
Edam
New Bra
Friulano Montasio
Emmental
Marble
Colby
Brick
Cheddar
Farmers
Skim Milk
Farmers Spiced
Fontina
Adam

Barnes Wines
Heritage Estates Bordeaux
   (Red)

Inniskillin
Marechal Foch (Red)
Millot Chamburtin (White)
Gamay Blanc (White)
Gamay Noir (Red)

Brights
Riesling (White)
Chardonnay (White)
Baco Noir (Red)
Spumante (Sparkling)
President Champagne
   (Sparkling)
Hostetter Trockenweiss
   (Sparkling)

Chateau-Gai
1982 Villard Noir (Red)
1982 Chancellor (Red)

CHEESE	WINE

Caraway
Smoked Hickory
Wine Cured Colby
Bacon
Herb & Garlic
Toasted Onion
Beer Cured
Sweet Pepper

Chateau des Charmes
Seyval Blanc (White)
Nokara Estate Chardonnay
  (White)
Estate Chardonnay (White)
Cour Rouge (Red)
Sentinel Rouge (Red)
Gamay Beaujolais (Red)

Andres
Richelieu (Sparkling)
Hochtaler (Sparkling)
Kurhauser Trocken Sekt
  (Sparkling)

Hillebrand
Etienne Brulé Blanc (White)
Gewürztraminer (White)

Dessert
Nippican (Cheddar with Port)
Cognac & Spice Cheddar
Kirsch Cheddar
Festival Gold (Cheddar with
  Ale)
Fruit & Nuts

Inniskillin
Late Harvest Riesling (White)
Muscat (White)
L'Allemand (White)

Brights
Hofstetter Trockenweiss
  (Sparkling)
Spumante (Sparkling)
President Cream Sherry
President Port

Chateau-Gai
LaMont Sparkling Dry White
  Wine

Chateau des Charmes
Late Harvest Estate (White)

Bread Baking

Though some of the flour used for baking comes from small, privately run mills, most of the flour – all-purpose, whole-wheat, instant-blending, and cake-and-pastry flour – comes from the Robin Hood Multi-Foods Mill in Port Colborne.
Is there a kitchen that does not contain a bag of this staff of life? Robin Hood is synonymous with baking. To prove that they care about our mental as well as physical well-being and to ensure results after all that mixing and kneading, they've come up with a neat checklist. Do any of the descriptions look familiar?

Description	Reason why	What to do
Bread is too small.	The oven was too hot or was too cold.	Check the temperature of the oven and place the pans in the oven so they are not touching to assure a good circulation of warm air. The dough should rise at room temperature (between 75 and 85 degrees F.)
Bread has a coarse texture and is crumbly.	a) Bread was allowed to rise too long. b) Too much kneading.	a) Let dough rise just until it is double in volume, at each rising. b) Knead until dough is smooth and elastic only.
Bread does not rise in the oven.	a) The rising period was too long. b) The oven was too hot and a crust formed on the bread before it had finished rising.	a) Do not let bread rise any more than double in volume. b) Make sure the oven temperature is correct.
Dough does not rise or rises too slowly.	a) The yeast is not active. b) The dough is cold. c) The ingredients used are too cold.	Use fresh yeast and test the water in which it is dissolved to make sure it is lukewarm. Water that is too hot will kill the yeast; water too cold will retard its action. Make sure that the dough rises in a warm place – between 70 and 85 degrees F, away from drafts but not overheated. Make sure all ingredients used are at room temperature.

Description	Reason why	What to do
Loaf is too big and poorly shaped.	a) The bread was allowed to rise too long in pan or too much dough was used for the size of the pan. b) Oven temperature too low.	a) The bread should not be allowed to rise more than double in volume. b) Check oven temperature.
Texture of the bread is close and the bread is heavy.	The bread did not rise enough before it was baked or rose too much and the cells collapsed.	The bread should rise until double in volume.
Top of the baked bread wrinkles and cracks.	The bread has been cooled in a draft.	When the bread has baked, turn out of the pans and cool on a wire rack, away from drafts.
There are heavy brown particles in the bread.	A crust formed on the dough while it was rising and was mixed in when the dough was formed into loaves.	Grease the top of the dough and cover during the rising period.
Bread loses its shape while cooling.	a) Not baked long enough. b) Oven temperature too low.	Test bread by turning out of pan and rapping bottom of loaf with knuckles. It should sound hollow and bottom and sides of loaf should be nicely browned.

Metric Conversions

In cooking, it is not possible to convert directly from one set of utensils to another, since the numbers do not work out to even measures in most cases. However, here are some approximate equivalents to apply when using metric utensils.

1 tsp. = approximately 5 mL
1 tbsp. = approximately 15 mL
¼ cup = approximately 60 mL
⅓ cup = approximately 80 mL
½ cup = approximately 115 mL
1 cup = approximately 225 mL

8-inch square pan × 2 inches deep = 20 × 5 cm
9-inch square pan × 2 inches deep = 22 × 5 cm
8-inch × 4-inch × 3-inch loaf pan = 20 × 10 × 7 cm
9-inch × 5-inch × 3-inch loaf pan = 22 × 12 × 7 cm
9-inch pie plate   = 22 × 4 cm

200°F. = 100°C
250°F. = 120°C
300°F. = 150°C
350°F. = 180°C
400°F. = 200°C
450°F. = 230°C

Index

Honey
    cake, Belgian (Zoetekock), 159
    cake, orange, 85
    mincemeat, green tomato, 83
Hors d'oeuvres. *See* Appetizers
Hot butter sauce, 58–59
Hot-fudge sauce, 43
Hot pickerel and wild-rice salad, 226
Hot-and-sour soup, 96–97

Icelandic brown bread, 146
Icelandic torte (Vineterta), 156–157
Icing
    almond-butter, 156–157
    cream cheese, 46
    maple syrup, 106
    yogurt, 51
Indian pudding, 38

Jam, carrot, 112–113
John's rum and raisin pie, 191

Kenora caboose, 231
Ketchup. *See* Tomato butter
Kidney(s)
    Mixed grill, English, 134–135
    Steak and, pie, 130–131
Kraut barracks (German cabbage
    squares), 152–153

Lake Nipissing
    caviar sauce, 179
    crispy fish in batter, 176–177
Lake Simcoe sweet and sour trout,
    127
Lamb
    mixed grill, English, 134–135
    roast, stuffed boneless, 108
    shepherd's pie, 90–91
Leek salad, warm potato-and-, 87
Leek, wild, and potato soup, 190–191
Lemon
    chicken baked in a bag, 65
    glaze, 50

Lemon (continued)
    meringue pie. *See* Loon Lake vine-
        gar pie
Linnanpaisti (Finnish sirloin-tip pot
    roast), 218
Liver, Calf's
    mixed grill, English, 134–135
Loaf, chocolate date, 48
Loon Lake vinegar pie, 189
Low-calorie
    Thousand Islands dressing, 145

Maple
    icing, -syrup, 106
    mousse, 107
    sweet potatoes, 106–107
Marinade(s)
    for bear, 208
    for beef, 203
    for buffalo, 203
    for suckling pig, 56–57
Marinated bear steaks, 208
Marinated buffalo roast, 203
Mayonnaise, garlic, 125
Measures, weights and, 243
Metric conversion chart, 243
Mincemeat
    chiffon pie, 84
    green tomato, 83
Mixed grill, English, 134–135
Molasses bread, 215
Mom's Welsh Spotted Dick (steamed
    pudding), 174
Monkey bread, cheddar, 27
Moose
    ground, 206–207
    roast in beer, 207
Mooseballs, sweet and sour, 206–207
Mousse, maple, 107
Mrs. Stitt's beet salad, 153
Mrs. Webber's spiced crab apples, 160
Muffins
    rice, 48–49
    whole-wheat pumpkin, 96

Printed in Canada